SURVIVING DISASTERS

and

FINDING GRACE

A Novel about Preparing to Live in a World

Without Electricity

SURVIVING DISASTERS
and
FINDING GRACE
A Novel about Preparing to Live in a World
Without Electricity

DARLENE MILLER

**PUBLICATION
CONSULTANTS**
WE BELIEVE IN THE POWER OF AUTHORS

PO Box 221974 Anchorage, Alaska 99522-1974
books@publicationconsultants.com—www.publicationconsultants.com

ISBN 978-1-63747-395-5
eISBN 978-1-63747-396-2
Library of Congress Catalog Card Number: 2024906847

Manufactured in the United States of America.

Acknowledgments

Thanks to Eta Chapman and Joan Pomeroy for their assistance with editing, suggestions, and proofing of this book. I also want to thank the sisters of Beta Sigma Phi Sorority for their suggestions on what they want in their homes to survive without electricity.

Introduction

A Novel about finding Family and Preparing to Live in a World Without electricity.

Surviving Disasters and Finding Grace is the novel of Karen, a young woman from California, who finds her Iowa family, except for her father, Joseph, and her sister, Grace. How does she find them? Or does she find them? That is the mystery.

The Iowa neighbor wants more than friendship as he assists Karen in finding her family. That is the romance.

When you use the definition of science-fiction as fiction based on an imagined future and major social and environmental changes, this book is also Science fiction. The family prepares for an imagined life without electricity. Are they able to survive in the countryside of the Midwest? A clue to this life is that they learn from their Amish and Mennonite neighbors.

Review: It is a remarkable book; the characters are brought to life in the foreground of history, romance, and how country folks survive major catastrophes. Karen finds her Iowa family, except for her father and sister. The mystery is how she finds them. Surviving a catastrophe is a lesson to all of us, although we cannot do it the same way as country folk. It was a good reminder to me. I finished the book with the feeling that I wish I could have tea with Grandma Rose.

Joan Pomeroy – author

Darlene Miller lives in rural Iowa when she is not traveling with her husband. Their RV has taken them to every state in the USA and to every province in Canada. Besides travel, Darlene likes reading, writing, gardening, and playing with her great-grandchildren.

She has written articles in such varied genres as *Escapees Magazine, Radiant Native Health, the Marion County Historical Newsletter, and Penwheels Magazine.*

Darlene's books include:

A Place in the Promised Land

RV Chuckles and Chuckholes – The Confessions of Happy Campers.

More RV Chuckles and Chuckholes – More Confessions of Happy Campers.

The Search for Grandma Sparkle- an Iowan mystery.

Callie and Natalie's Dutch Family History – with over 90 colored photos.

Elijah and Emma Meet Friends and Visit History – a story & coloring book.

Chapter 1

The young blonde woman, Karen Wells, stood near the baggage turntable in the Des Moines airport looking nervously for the cousin she was supposed to meet. She dug into her purse hunting for her cell phone. No, there wasn't a message.

She connected to the contact number of her cousin, Ryan Boender, but the phone was answered by a woman. The woman only said, "Hello."

Nervously, Karen answered, "This is Karen Wells. Is this the number I'm supposed to call for the ride to the Boender Farm?"

"Yes, I'm Ryan's mother, Betty Boender. I'm in the cell phone parking lot. Go outside. Stay in the boarding area and I'll pick you up." . . . "What are you wearing?"

"I have a red t-shirt with flowers on it and jeans. I'm carrying a red tote bag with my luggage. What kind of car are you driving so I can recognize you?"

"It's a grey Chevy."

Karen made her way to open the heavy door of the airport and met a heavy blast of humid air. She waited and waited.

Finally, a grey Chevy sedan pulled to the loading area.

"Are you Karen Wells?" The 50ish black haired woman asked.

"Yes, I'm Karen. Are you Ryan's mother?"

"Yes, don't loiter," she answered sharply. "Put your suitcase in the back seat and hop in. The wind is blowing. It is chilly out today."

When Karen left San Diego, it was a hundred degrees. Somehow, sixty – five degrees felt good for this spring day.

As Betty and Karen rode from the airport in Des Moines on Highway 5 to Betty and George's home near Albia, Iowa, Betty talked about the rest of the family.

"Our son, Ryan, couldn't pick you up because my husband, George, insisted that he and his college friend, Jack, help with the haying today. The forecast is for rain, so they need to get the hay in the barn.

"My daughter, Ann, is in Iowa City where she is taking classes to be an RN.

"My mother-in-law, Rose, is currently living in our house. I don't know how long she will be there, but it makes a problem with where you will sleep because she is in Ann's room."

A red pickup truck sped around them then slowed down to the speed limit in front of them. Betty's long black hair swished across her face when she turned her head toward her husband's niece. When Betty looked ahead, she slammed on the brakes.

Karen gasped at the near hit. "You almost rear - ended that red pickup. Please watch where you are going. Do you want me to drive?"

Betty answered, "No, I just don't know what to do." She brushed a tear from her cheek before putting both hands on the wheel. "No. I need to get away from George and his mother."

Karen said, "I thought she lived in an apartment of her own?"

"No," Betty answered. "The old lady moved in with us."

"When did that happen?" questioned Karen.

"A few weeks ago." Betty replied.

Karen said, "I don't understand. I thought that she moved out after George's dad died so you two could move onto the farm and take care of it. . . .When was that?"

"Three years ago. But six weeks ago, Rose fell going down the steps of her apartment, spent a few days in the hospital with a broken right hip, and went to live in a care facility."

The grey Chevy came to a stop at the intersection of Highway 92 and Highway 5 and turned east past fields of corn and soy beans. They traveled east around Knoxville. Then they turned south toward Albia.

They were quiet for about thirty miles until Karen became uncomfortable with the silence. She didn't want to talk about the relationship between Betty and Rose, so she changed the subject.

"Look at that large, beautiful garden. The flowers are beautiful and it looks like vegetables are starting to grow. There isn't a weed in sight."

Betty said, "That's an Amish homestead. There are many in this part of Iowa, especially near Moravia. The Amish and Mennonites live mostly on garden produce, but also eat meat.

"They are pretty backward, since most of them only attended eight grades of school.

"The Amish and some of the Mennonites don't use electricity which makes keeping house very labor intensive."

"There are so many buildings!" Karen said with surprise.

"Yes." Betty said. "They need buildings for all their animals and for the grandparents. When the grandparents are too old to farm, they build a small house for the old ones, and have their son and his wife move into the big house.

"Didn't you know that your mother and Rose were Amish? Pete was Dutch. He fell in love with Rose when they met at a church gathering. Of course, the Amish held church in each other's houses, but there was a graduation reception, or some other gathering, in the Methodist Church basement. Rose and her family made the deserts and catered the gathering.

"The Amish don't have a church building. They meet in each other's home for worship so Rose got married in her parents' house.

"Rose and Pete were a compatible couple. They both were home bodies, liked growing things, ate home cooked food, and saved everything."

Karen changed the subject. "It won't be hard for Ann to get a job as a nurse, but is there a hospital near you?"

Betty answered, "There is a hospital in Albia, but I doubt that Ann will be living close to us, when she gets her degree and nursing license.

"We continue to have the tradition that everyone comes home once a month on the first Sunday of the month to celebrate birthdays. Holidays are celebrated at the traditional times. Ann usually comes home for our celebrations."

Betty continued on the subject of Rose. "No one picked up Rose at the last Sunday dinner. She said that she felt 'left out.' Grandma Rose complains all the time!

"She has to call for help when she needs to go to the bathroom because of fall precautions, that the center required, but it takes the aides as much as fifteen minutes to come to assist her. Then it is too late and she has soiled herself, so they put her in diapers, which she hates. Another client, named Dorothy, comes in her room without permission and steals her lotion or anything that Dorothy wants. Rose's complaints go on and on.

"Anyway, Rose phoned and asked for George to bring her some special shampoo and lotion. She cried and told George that she hates it at the nursing home so George brought his mother home, to move in with us, without asking me. I feel like telling him it is either her or me.

"Rose really drives me crazy! It isn't my house anymore. It's hers."

Karen commented, "But wasn't it her house for forty - five years? I think Ryan said that they moved onto the farm right after they got married. I thought that Ryan's grandmother was in an apartment. That's what Ryan told me. . . . What happened?"

Betty explained. "After Rose fell and broke her hip, she was taken to a Carter's Care Facility. She hated it there. She says that they wake her up before 7 in the morning and take her to breakfast in her pajamas. They have eggs every morning. She is allergic to eggs so they give her green juice from a blender and a piece of toast. She wants cereal with fruit.

"After she is dressed, they schedule her to participate in exercises. They assist her to shower, whenever they feel like it, but it is every three days. Then she sits for hours and hours with nothing to do but watch television.

"She drives me crazy. It isn't my house anymore. She wants to 'help'. When she puts dishes away, they are not put in the cupboard where they are supposed to go. I'm forever hunting for them. She washed my blouses in hot water and shrunk them in the dryer. She even takes my toilet paper and puts it on the spindle so the paper rolls under instead of over. Everyone knows that toilet paper needs to roll over."

Chapter 2

Rose pushed her walker into the living room of the house that now belonged to Betty and George.

"I think that the brown living room sofa should be under the window where I had it sitting when I lived here." she thought. She plopped down into the new recliner that Betty bought for George. *"I wonder if my recliner is in storage since I'm no longer living at Carter Health Care. It belonged to my husband, Pete, but since he died it felt so good to me. It smelled like his after shave and it almost felt like he was putting his arms around me. . . . Now what can I do to help Betty for supper? She will be tired after getting my granddaughter, Karen, from the airport."*

Rose released the lever on George's reclining chair, and rose from it by holding on to the arms of the chair, to push herself up. She grabbed the walker and hobbled to the kitchen to look for ingredients for a meal.

The kitchen was the same as when she lived here, except Ellen had a new refrigerator, freezer, and an electric stove, but they were in the same places as her old appliances. You had to look closely to see that they were different from the old ones. Even most of the utensils were in the same drawers as Rose had placed them.

She sat on a stool, by the counter, and peeled four potatoes and one half of an onion, and placed them in the bottom of a 9 x 7 baking pan. In the refrigerator, she found six cube steaks that were almost thawed. She browned the cube steaks in the frying pan. Then, she placed the cubed beef steaks on top of the potato and onion mixture. Next, she covered the whole thing with milk and cream of mushroom soup. The casserole was placed in the 350 - degree oven.

"I think that the perennial lilies that I planted on the west side of the house, would look lovely with Betty's dishes. I'm so glad that Betty didn't destroy them like she did the flowers in the front yard. Rose found her favorite vase in the cupboard in the laundry room, and placed the cut orange and yellow day lilies from the flower bed into it.

Rose saw the grey Chevy after it stopped in the driveway. She hurried to the door and opened her arms to hug Karen. Karen placed her suitcase inside the foyer, and responded with a hug and then a kiss on her grandmother's wrinkled cheek.

Karen asked "What is the wonderful smell? You have beautiful lilies on the table too." Rose beamed at the greeting from Karen.

In a cold voice, Betty yelled, "What have you done? I wanted the beef cubed steaks for lunch tomorrow. I smell onions too. You know that Ryan doesn't like onions. Look at the mess you made in my kitchen! Just go to your room! I'll call you when dinner is ready!"

Rose brushed a tear from her face, as she silently turned to go to her bedroom.

Karen waited a few minutes in the living room until she decided to go knock on the door behind the living room where her grandmother had disappeared.

"Is it okay if I come in?" she asked.

"Yes, child, come in," her grandmother invited her. "Sit beside me in that chair."

Karen said, "I hope that you can tell me about my parents. It is important to me to find my roots. Maybe I can find out just who I am."

Grandma Rose answered. "Your great grandparents, Mary and John, were Amish who moved to this farm from Ohio.

Their only child was Peter. I married Pete. Our children are Ellen, and George, and Alice. Alice was married to Joseph Miller. They had two children, you and Jim.

"I think there is a photo of the four of you in the attic." Grandma Rose added, "I insisted on the photo when a photographer was here for George and my 25th wedding anniversary, but I didn't display it, because your parents reluctantly posed for it. Their bishop says that it is against their religion to pose for photos."

Karen became excited. "Oh, I would love to see it. I even want a copy of it."

After a minute, Karen asked. "What happened to my mother?"

"Alice died of an infection a month after giving birth to you. Joe, your father, was devastated. It was as though his spirit left him too. He was on auto pilot. He responded to others, when they talked to him, in as few words as possible. He did what anyone told him when he was asked to help with chores, but he didn't play with Jim and didn't even want to hold you.

"Ellen was married to Matthew, but had no children of their own. Peter was twenty - five and married to me. I was in an auto accident and was bed - bound in the hospital. I was pregnant with Ann and had three-year-old Ryan. It was in the middle of winter and everyone was having a hard time. I had problems with my pregnancy, so I was put on bed rest. After five months, I came home. My friend, Esther, was caring for me and keeping house. I couldn't even go to my daughter's funeral.

"Agnes, Joe's mother, said that he couldn't work and care for Jim and a new baby. It was an answer to prayer for Ellen. She couldn't have children and wanted them badly so, after Alice's funeral, she took you and Jim to California to live with her and Matthew. Matt was so glad to have a son, but this was supposed to be a temporary thing."

Karen responded, "Aunt Ellen treated me like a daughter. I don't know why she and Matt didn't adopt me."

16

Rose answered, "I don't think that Joseph wanted to sign the papers. He always thought that he would remarry and have you and Jim live with him."

Karen said, "I remember a man coming to California with a pretty lady. I must have been only three-years-old then. Ellen said that they were going to visit us from Iowa, where she used to live, but I saw her crying after she told us that they were coming to visit."

Rose said "Ellen was afraid that they were going to take you back to Iowa. Katie saw how you loved your Aunt Ellen and Uncle Matt. You were excited to begin pre-school with your friends and Jim was happy to graduate from the Kindergarten Center and go to the "big school." Katie told her new husband, that she thought it best if you both remained with Ellen and Matt. She didn't know anything about raising young children, since she was an only child. Joseph was heartbroken, but he reluctantly agreed. He was still very upset when he came back to the farm.

"Katie was from Chicago, so she had never lived on a farm. This farm is a dairy farm. At that time, George and Joe milked 30 cows. All daily activities were planned around the morning and late afternoon milking. That winter, snow came early. Of course, the cows were kept in the barn to keep them safe and warm. That meant hay and feed had to be fed to the cows and manure had to be shoveled out. This was the season that any repairs to farm equipment had to be made, so of course, Joe spent most of his time in the barn. Katie couldn't stand the smelly barn. She felt shut in with cabin fever."

"What's cabin fever?" asked Karen.

Rose responded, "You aren't physically ill, but depressed because snow storms make it impossible to keep the roads open, so you stay indoors and don't go anywhere.

"About a week before Christmas, Katie said she was lonesome for her parents. Joe drove her to the train station in Ottumwa and she took the train to Chicago. A day after New Year's Day, Katie phoned Joe and told him that she was pregnant and wanted to stay with her mother. Joe had two choices. He could either stay on the farm or move into her parent's house with her."

"What did he do?" Karen questioned.

"He moved to Chicago. He never wrote or phoned. Whenever I called, he was not available. Katie sent a baby card to us, announcing the birth of Grace Elizabeth Miller in July. I sent her the infant clothes from my daughter, Ann. I also made Grace a dozen baby diapers from white flannel and sent them, but I never heard from Katie again. The letters that I sent to Joe were returned. I never heard from any of them again. George took a trip to Chicago and stopped at Katie's parent's home but the maid told him that she didn't know a Joe Miller and wouldn't let George into the house."

Chapter 3

Ryan and his friend, Jack, hurried from the barn into the house and went straight to the bathroom to wash up for supper and comb their hair.

"What's for supper?" Ryan asked.

His mom answered, "Your grandmother made pork chops and potatoes. I made a salad. Go tell your grandmother and Karen that supper is ready. They are in Ann's bedroom."

Ryan knocked on the door, then opened it and announced, "Supper is ready." Karen and Grandma Rose hurried to the table.

Karen looked more closely at the two men sitting at the table. They were both close to six feet tall, with bodies that her friends would call "hunks". She supposed that the speaker was her cousin, Ryan. He had baby blue eyes while the other man had dark hair and deep brown eyes. *"Who was this other man who looked at her so intently?"*

"Hi, Karen. This is my neighbor and friend, Jack." Ryan turned to Jack and saw that Jack's eyes were sparkling and it seemed that he didn't know what to say.

Karen was surprised when Grandma Rose reached over on both sides of her and held both Karen and Ryan's hand. No one prayed before a meal in her house in California.

Grandma said, "It's my turn to pray tonight. Dear God, thank you for this beautiful day and for bringing my grandchild safely here to visit us. Thank you for this food. Be with us and help us to do your will. In Jesus name we pray. Amen."

Jack was quiet during supper. He looked at his food, but it seemed as though whenever he looked up, he was staring at Karen who was seated across the table from him. She smiled at him and then looked away.

Jack said, "I've known Ryan for most of my life, but I didn't know that he had a cousin living in California."

"I didn't know that either." Ryan replied. "I found out when some guys from college decided to get their genealogy done. I was afraid because I didn't want the guys to know that my grandmother was really Amish. But since we are the same coloring, I didn't think anyone would know. I didn't know about Karen. Then I received a notice that my DNA was most like a woman in San Diego. I asked my dad about it and he told me of cousins who lived in San Diego."

Karen answered, "When Ryan shared with me his information, I asked my mom about it. Ellen was upset but told me that she was really my aunt. She didn't give me many details but confirmed that Ryan was probably my cousin from Iowa. Ryan got my phone number and called me. Since school is out for the summer, I asked if I could come to visit and learn more about my family."

"Are you still in college?" Betty asked Karen.

"No. I teach fourth grade."

Ryan rose from the chair and turned to his mother, "Is it okay if I sleep in the camper tonight? The barn is too smelly. Do you want to join me, Jack?"

"Whatever you want to do," Betty answered.

Jack answered, "It's okay with me. That way I won't wake Mom up when we get an early start on haying. . . You do have heating and air conditioning in the camper, don't you?"

"You bet. It's even better than my room. Come on, help me milk the cows." Ryan said to Jack.

"Rose, you do the dishes, I'm going to lie down a bit, since I have a headache," Betty instructed.

Karen started to pick up the dishes and said. "I'll help with the dishes."

"Just leave them on the table when you are through," Betty instructed. "I'll put them away, so I will know where to find them."

They were alone while they were doing the dishes, so Karen started the conversation with her grandmother. "I think it is fascinating that my relatives were Amish. Were you brought up in an Amish family, or was it your husband?

"I was brought up Amish," Her grandmother answered.

"Are there very many Amish around here?" Karen asked.

"Yes. I only visit a few, but George and Ryan are very friendly with them. Ryan took his horse to them to be serviced. After the colt was born, it was the Amish who trained it. They ask George to drive them when they want to go places that are too far for their horses to go and return in a day. George has also driven them to medical facilities, such as Iowa City Hospitals.

"If you are observant, you will see places with clothes lines, large gardens, and horses in the fields or in a pasture. They can usually ride their horse and buggies on the side of the road because the shoulders are very wide. The men wear suspenders on their pants while the women wear long dresses even on the hottest of days. The women sew the clothing, so you may see several children wearing the same brown or gray clothing made from the same material. The girls wear long hair while the boys have Dutch - boy cuts. It looks like someone put a bowl on their heads and cut around it. You never see children in shorts. They may be bare footed though."

"The children don't wear shoes?" Karen questioned.

"Oh, they wear shoes to school and for religious services in their homes. Shoes are also worn in the winter, but seldom in the summer. It saves on the leather.

"Your mother made a nice blue dress for her wedding to your father."

Karen stopped washing the plate and turned to look at her grandmother. "I thought you said that you followed the

21

English ways after you married and raised your children by English ways. Why didn't she wear a white dress?"

"Because your father was Amish and Alice joined the church and promised to follow the Amish way of life."

Karen asked, "Betty said that you grew up Amish. Were you shunned when you married George?"

Rose answered. "There wasn't a formal shunning, since I was in my rumspringa years and had not joined the church. I joined the Methodist church in Forest Grove, so George and I could attend together. George preferred the Christian Reformed Church but there wasn't that church near us."

Rose continued. "It was a huge blow to my father's ego that his daughter would leave the Amish faith. He never spoke to me much, after I married. He loved Alice and the fact that Alice was going to be confirmed in the Amish church.

"My mother came to visit when my father was busy. She would hold my babies and talk about recipes but she couldn't understand how to use an electric mixer or a modern stove.

"Many of my friends couldn't understand why I liked listening to the radio or television. Over time, visits with my mother occurred less and less often.

Karen asked, "Do you believe in God or Jesus?"

Grandma Rose answered, "Both of them, plus the Holy Spirit. They are one being called the Trinity. I believe in the Bible and try to live a Christian life. I would like you to come to church with us on Sunday to learn more about our religion."

Karen answered. "I would love to go with you."

Chapter 4

George took off his shoes in the doorway as he entered his house. "Hello Everybody. What's for supper?"

Grandma Rose looked at the floor. Betty coughed to clear her throat. Karen smiled and said, "Aunt Betty made mashed potatoes and green beans. Grandma Rose made pork chops."

George answered, "Then supper will be good. Betty is a good cook and Mom makes good pork chops. The smell is delicious."

Rose could have kissed George but instead she just smiled. "We can eat as soon as the table is set."

During the supper conversation, Ryan said, "I think that Grandma Rose needs more space than her room. Don't you think it's a great idea to build her a small house?"

Betty said, "I guess that she could use the camper, but what happens when we have the family reunion at Rathburn Lake on the 4th of July?"

Rose answered, "I'd have problems going up and down the steps with my bum legs and knees."

Karen added, "When we went past an Amish farm, the grandparents had their own little house. Some of the manufactured houses are small yet very efficient."

George said, "Let's pray and think about it."

Surviving Disasters and Finding Grace

The next day, after George finished his work in the field, he went to see his mother. She was in Ann's bedroom, sewing a button on one of his shirts.

Rose said, "I have been thinking about this house. I would love to have a small house again. I can get up and eat when I feel like it. I can watch what I wish on TV and go to bed without bothering anyone. Can I have lots of storage space? Maybe you can even rototill a space on the east side of the house so I can grow a few flowers and vegetables."

"That's settled then. I'll look at blueprints and get materials and have us a house raising on Wednesday after the 4th of July when the family is here to help. Maybe we can have our Amish friends help us. They would like a little cash. I'll go tell Betty what we have decided."

George went to Betty and announced, "We are going to build a tiny house for Mom after the 4th of July when the family is here."

Betty voice was shrill as she answered, "Without talking to me about it? . . . What will I have to do about food?"

"I hoped that would make you happy!"

After hearing the loud voices, Rose entered the living room. "Please don't shout. We will have pot luck for food."

Betty sighed and said, "She has the last word again."

Betty added, "We will have to have some rules about living close together."

The next day, George thought and thought about what would make his mother happy. He decided that Rose needed to feel useful. If she was busy, Betty would be happier too.

While they were in the barn, doing the afternoon milking, George brought up the subject with Ryan. "Since it's still the first week in June, and the house won't be finished until the middle or end of July; my mom needs to keep busy with a project. What do you think about us putting in a garden?"

Ryan said, "That would be great. I love fresh food."

George replied, "Would you talk to Grandma Rose about it? Are you willing to be the one to help her?"

"Sure, Dad." Ryan replied.

After supper, Ryan walked to the patio behind the Boender house. He saw Grandma Rose sitting alone. "Hi. I think that I will join you for a while." Ryan sat down beside his grandmother.

They looked at the green grass under the tall oak trees, and the fields of corn that were just peeping up in rows in the field. A rabbit and several barn swallows looked for food just ten feet away from them. If you were quiet enough, you could hear water flowing over the rocks in the creek below the hill. Since the highway was on the other side of the house, they felt like they were in a private paradise.

"Isn't this a beautiful day that God has made?" Rose said.

Suddenly, a young buck deer bounded over the hill. They watched the graceful, fluid movement of the deer as he moved horizontally across the top of the hill.

"He probably got scared by Jack and Karen," Ryan said. "They are bicycling along the path by the creek. I think Jack is sweet on Karen. He asked if he could borrow my bike and have Karen use Ann's bike to follow the creek path. I was clearly not invited."

Grandma decided to change the subject. "I love to see things grow. I wish that I could have a garden with vegetables and flowers."

"Dad and I were just talking about that. Why can't you? I can make waist high boards like you see in a greenhouse and help you prepare it. We can put some flowers in pots and the rest in the ground. Then you can watch it grow."

Grandma Rose added, "I want to have tomatoes. The tomatoes you buy in the store don't taste the same."

"They sure don't. Mom says that a garden is too much work and you can buy vegetables quite cheaply."

Grandma Rose spoke, "I like fresh vegetables. I can help the family by providing fresh food."

Ryan said. "If mom doesn't like it, I'll come over to eat with you.

Ryan went into his grandmother's house to get paper and a pencil from her desk to plot out the garden.

After he returned to the patio, Ryan said, "Dad said to put the garden behind the barn so it won't get trampled when your house is being built. Next year, we can put it behind your house. Do we need to fence it in so the rabbits and deer don't feast on it?"

Grandma Rose answered, "It will be easier for me to use the walker if I don't have to worry about a gate. Rabbits won't be able to climb up to the elevation of the raised garden. We can plant zinnias in a pot at the ends of the garden to discourage them. They don't like the smell of zinnias.

Grandma added. "I want to grow green beans, squash and peppers too. It's too late to plant potatoes, onions, and lettuce this year. They like cool weather. It will be a swell garden."

She stood up and kissed Ryan on the cheek. "It's my bedtime. I'll dream about the garden and my new house tonight. Now, I have so much to look forward to. Thanks so much for your help."

Chapter 5

Grandma Rose was so excited about her new house and garden plans, that she could hardly sleep. The next morning, she phoned her friend, Esther, to tell her the news.

Esther was very happy for her friend. "Why don't I pick you up and we can buy plants and talk more about gardens?"

Rose answered, "That would be great! Is it too late, in the season, to plant seeds?"

"Yes, gardens in this area should be planted by May 15, but many vegetable plants will still grow if they are planted soon. On the way to the Home and Garden Shop, we can discuss it more. Also, you will want to look at my garden."

Esther continued, "How about it if I drive over to pick you up at one? Will you finish lunch by then?"

"Yes. I'll see you then."

Rose was ready when she saw Esther's old Ford pull up in the driveway. Using her cane, she hobbled to the car.

Esther jumped out of her car, gave Rose a hug, and opened the car door for her.

Rose said, "It's been four years since I planted anything. What tips do you have for a garden?"

Esther responded. "I plant basil, beside my tomato plants. It is good in tomato sauce and seems to keep tomato worms away. Cucumbers grow well near tomatoes."

She continued, "This year I saved my egg cartons and used them for seed – starting trays. I pick holes in the bottom of the carton for drainage. Then I cut the top of the cartons off, and place it underneath, to catch excess soil and water. I add soil and seeds and I'm ready to go.

"Do you remember the old aquarium that I used to have in my living room? I put it on my back patio. I placed some old boards on the bottom. The seed – starters went on top of the boards. I closed the lid and turned on the light. When the lid is closed, the inside air is humid. After the seeds sprout, I opened the lid to circulate fresh air. I opened and closed it until the plants were too tall to keep the lid closed. Then, I removed the boards. In April, I alternated keeping the lid open during the day and closed at night, to insulate the seedlings from freezing temperatures."

At the Home and Garden Shop, Rose bought tomato, cucumber, squash, and pepper plants. Then they traveled to Esther's house, where Esther showed Rose the plants that she had grown from seed. The plants that were the same as what Rose now owned, except Esther had also planted peas, green beans, beets, and onions.

Rose could hardly wait to show her new plants to Ryan and George, but Esther served Rose tea and cookies, before driving her home.

On the ride to George's house, Rose said, "I will be glad to help you can your vegetables. I can do a lot of work, as long as I'm sitting down."

Esther answered, "I'll be glad for the help, especially with snapping green beans and shelling peas.

- - - - - - - - - - - - - - - - -

Rose sat by the window of the main house to watch the neighbors, which included the Amish, help her relatives assemble her new home. The Amish helped each other when they needed to build so they were very knowledgeable and organized at carpentry. They also worked for "Englishers" for pay because the Amish needed money to buy supplies from outsiders.

It was amazing how fast the little house took shape. The rafters were laid out on the lawn and lifted in place by ten men on each side. Before long the box of the house was braced and standing. The roof boards and shingles were added. Then the box of the house was divided into a great room, enclosed bedroom and bathroom. Cupboards were placed on one end of the great room and became the kitchen. The bathroom door opened to both the bedroom and the great room. The bathroom had a walk in shower with a chair, a sink and a commode.

Rose wanted "lots of storage." The east and south walls of the bedroom became closets with hangers for her clothes and shelves for books on the east side while the other closet was made with shelves for plastic boxes "to hold stuff."

Since most of the house was open, it appeared more spacious than it really was. That made it easier for a handicapped person to move around if Rose ever needed a wheel chair. A crawl space had been dug before the house was assembled with cement blocks as a foundation to hold up the house. Then they placed the two handicapped approved thirty – six – inch - wide outside doors level to the ground and handicapped approved.

Outside, to feed the workers, boards were placed on sawhorses to make tables. Sheets became tablecloths. Then the slow cookers were placed on one end loaded with pulled pork, ground beef, and chicken. Buns and potato dishes were in the middle putting the salads and vegetable dishes on the other end. It took another table to hold all the cakes, pies and other deserts.

Even with taking an hour out to eat, the shell of the house was finished by nightfall. Now it needed plumbing, wiring, insulation and sheet rock. The flooring came next and then the cupboards, mirror, lavatory, and commode were placed in the bathroom. George and his son finished these tasks in a few days.

Rose said she wanted the bedroom and the bathroom to be "robin's eggshell blue and the great room to be ivory." After

Karen helped with the painting, the tiny house was ready for the furniture and kitchen stuff from the storage unit. Rose was so thankful that everything had not been sold or given to the big house but she remembered that the new brown sofa was not hers anymore.

Yes, Pete's recliner was there and placed where Rose could watch TV, but she said that she would rather read a book. A table and lamp were placed by the recliner for her. Sheets were placed on the bed, so she was ready for sleep. But before she slept, she went to her box of makeup and perfume and got the can of Old Spice aftershave that Pete used to use and sprayed the recliner to remind her of her husband.

After a mere two weeks of construction, the house was complete, ready to be lived in.

The Amish thought of the house, that they helped build, as *"Daadi Haus."* This meant "grandparent's house."

George thought of the house as, *"Boender Bungalow."*

Betty thought of the house as, *"Rose's Place."*

Ryan thought of the house as, *"Gradma Roses's Cabin."*

Karen thought of the house *as, "Tiny House."*

Grandma Rose thought of the house as, *"Home."*

Chapter 6

George played a fair game of golf but the best part of the day was lunch afterwards with the guys. Their camaraderie was evident to anyone who saw the foursome sitting at the table in the clubhouse.

John, in his mid-sixties, was the youngest. His most distinguishing features were the slivery wave in his bushy hair and the tan mark on his forehead, which showed the line from his hat. He looked like a farmer in his jeans and chambray shirt.

David wore khaki pants and a button down shirt, cowboy boots and a Stetson. He looked the part of a good old boy who sold insurance before he retired. The hat served the purpose of covering his baldness, but maybe it was to protect his head from the sun.

Mark's thin hair was mostly white with a few dark spots in the back. He was a retired policeman who preferred polyester pants, a button down shirt and a light jacket. Probably, the jacket was to cover his weapon, which he carried in the small of his back.

George had a comb over to cover the baldness on the top of his head. He wore jeans and a t-shirt with the symbol of the Albia High School Blue Demons on it.

After showering and changing clothes, they stored their golf clubs and spiked golf shoes in the lockers. They unanimously agreed to have lunch at the club house.

While eating their salads, David remarked, "I wonder how the football team will do this year. Remember the Albia game vs. Centerville 2022 on Sep 2? I hope they do better this year."

"Yeah," Mark said. "Wasn't the score something like 24 to 0? Albia won, but the football team hasn't been the same since Ryan played in it. What is he doing this summer?"

"He is helping me milk the cows and bring in the hay," George answered. "He got interested in his genealogy and found a cousin from California who is visiting us now."

Their steaks and baked potatoes arrived.

The talk went to how much rain they had two days ago.

David remarked that a friend from Raleigh, North Carolina, was sending him messages about a coming doomsday. "The world will change after an EMP shuts off all electricity for months or even years, Joe tells me. What would we do?"

"What's an EMP?" John asked. David answered, "It is an electrical magnetic pulse. It can be caused by a nuclear bomb above our country or an enormous solar flare. One hundred and fifty years ago, on Sept. 2, 1859, the Carrington Event triggered a geomagnetic storm on Earth. The explosion blew out a coronal mass ejection that blasted our planet with high-speed gusts of super-heated plasma clouds, which had magnetic fields embedded in them.

"The storm produced intense aurora displays much further south than the northern lights can usually be seen. It also caused fires as the enhanced electric current flowing through telegraph wires ignited recording tape at telegraph stations.

"If it happened today, a storm on the scale of the Carrington event, would affect all the electricity in the country as well as cause an internet apocalypse, sending large numbers of people and businesses offline.

"An EMP does weird things to machinery, like shorting it out. We would be back in the dark ages. A nuclear attack above our country could do the same thing. How would we survive?"

"Everyone's first problem would be getting enough food to survive," John answered. "I have corn and soybeans and a garden. Margie has lots of canned food from last year's produce," he added. "We even have 6-year-old canned jars of fruits and vegetables that Aunt Tilly willed us."

Mark asked, "How did that happen?"

"Aunt Tilly was proud of her cooking and canning. She didn't have any children so she willed us her 'canning jars-empty and full.' The money from the sale of the farm went to her church. We really didn't know what to do with this inheritance but Margie found space in the basement to store it. Sometimes she opens a can of peaches and makes a cobbler with them and I can't tell know the difference between canned peaches from the store and the old stuff." He laughed. "We didn't really appreciate the food. It's funny that Aunt Tilly's food may save us."

George responded, "We have a generator and solar power in case the electricity fails us after a storm, so I can milk the cows, but we would probably have to eventually kill the cows for meat. Generators run on gasoline and I don't know how long that would last. Since gas and diesel pumps are operated by electricity, you couldn't get gasoline if pumps were not operating. How would the milk get delivered to the dairy?"

Mark responded, "I'm concerned with safety. Everyone around here knows you have a dairy. Looters may be desperate to steal milk for their children or even shoot your cows. Corn can be ground into flour and baked on a grill. Soy beans can be soaked and cooked if you can get propane from your large propane tank. I guess that you may have to use wood if the gas was depleted."

Mark continued, "Jill and I would be okay for a while. We would just live in the RV. I usually have a full tank of water so we can leave whenever we get hitch fever. Both the clean and dirty tanks are empty. Our refrigerator and stove run on propane. We even have a propane heater. We usually save on water by putting a basin in the sink and using that water to flush the toilet."

David said, "Insurance wouldn't help you because all accounts would be electronic and we couldn't access them. Banks would be closed. I guess you could meet with neighbors or other church members and barter. You couldn't pay your bills because no one would know what you owed. You could also have cash on hand but I'm not sure what the value of the currency would be. You can't eat money."

John remarked, "Remember that many towns in Iowa were built around coal mines. There was a coal mine behind my acreage. There is probably still coal there. We could get some coal out for heat and cooking. You can see some coal in the ditches on Highway G -17 where the Wilcox mine was."

David said, "My friend suggested that I build a Faraday box for any electronics that I'm not using."

"What's that?" asked George.

David answered. "A Faraday box is used to block electromagnetic fields. It is formed by a covering of conductive material or a combination of metals to soak up the EMP and divert the pulse from whatever you put in the box. The object you put in the box cannot touch the inside of the box. You can make a Faraday box from extra strength aluminum foil but absolutely no light can enter the box. You need to wrap a cardboard box several times in the foil and then tape the seams.

"Another item you can use is a microwave oven. They are usually built to protect the user from rays. The microwave in your camper is an example of a useful tool, but don't have the microwave plugged in."

George asked, "Do you think that my metal pole barn would act as a Faraday Box, since it is metal and has a dirt floor as a ground?"

David answered, "I don't know. You would have to seal all light from your two windows and any seams in the building and then maybe it could work."

"You, George, could be better prepared than most of us since you have a well and septic system."

George answered, "I don't believe an EMP will come in my lifetime."

The men had finished their meal so they rose to go to their cars.

Mark added, "My friend in Moravia is the most prepared. He is Amish and has never used electricity."

Chapter 7

George thought about the conversation he had with his golf buddies on the way home from Albia. When he stopped his 2020 Ford 150 pickup in the gravel driveway, he saw that it was almost time to milk the cows but on entering the barn he saw that Ryan and Jack were already busy pouring milk into the huge cooler.

"It looks like you boys want something." George mumbled.

"They're showing a movie in the King theater in Albia," Ryan answered. "We want to borrow the Chevy."

"Why don't you take your pick up? Is it out of gas?" George queried.

"Jack wouldn't mind being squeezed in with Karen, but I think she will be more comfortable in the Chevy." Ryan teased.

Jack's face turned red but he didn't answer.

Ryan added, "We want to take the car to the Liberty Cemetery tomorrow too. Karen wants to see her mother's grave."

"First, ask your mother if she needs the car," George answered.

When Ryan and Jack finished milking the next morning, they hurried into the house to get breakfast and saw that Karen was already finished cooking the bacon, eggs and toast.

"Isn't this a beautiful day that God has made?" Karen greeted them.

"You sound like Grandma Rose." Ryan teased.

Karen ignored Ryan's teasing. "I wonder why you call your grandmother, Grandma Rose, instead of Granny or Nana or some of the other names for grandmother."

Ryan answered, "Because she asked Ann and me to call her by both names. Dad's mother was still alive when I was small, so she was Grandma Boender. Jack's grandmother was Grandma Welsh, even though we were not related. When we were at a church social, I called, "Grandma." Several women said, "Yes?"

"I was embarrassed because I needed help to go to the bathroom. Grandma Rose then told me to call her by both names so everyone would know who I meant. Ann and I have always called her Grandma Rose since that time."

Karen answered. "Okay. I talked to Grandma Rose early this morning. and she wants to go with us to the cemetery. I wonder if she has awakened."

Ryan answered, "Grandma Rose is up with the birds."

Ryan looked at Jack with a grin and said, "Grandma likes to sit in the front seat because it is more comfortable for her legs," Then he added. "Do you want to drive or sit with Karen in the back seat?"

"You'd better drive. It's your family car." Jack replied.

Karen didn't respond to the conversation but thought that sitting next to Jack would be nice.

"I'll go tell Grandma Rose that we are ready." Karen said.

Karen went out the back door carefully. *"If the door slams it will wake Ellen,"* she thought.

She knocked on the door of Grandma Rose's tiny house.

The older woman responded to Karen's greeting with, "Isn't it a beautiful day that God has made?"

"I'm not so sure about that," Karen answered. "The weather report said that we may have a storm."

"You may be right. My knees always tell me when a storm is brewing, and they are telling me so. . . .Are the boys ready?"

"Yeah, they said to get you."

"Okay, I haven't been off the farm for a few days," Grandma Rose answered. "Let me grab a sweater and my umbrella. I'll be along in a few minutes."

Ryan opened the door of the car and helped Grandma Rose into the front seat. Then he put the walker and umbrella in the trunk of the car. Jack opened the door of the car and held it open for Karen. "*That's nice,*" thought Karen. "*Jack is a gentleman.*"

"We'd better hurry before the storm," Ryan declared. "The cemetery is on a rock road that doesn't have much rock on it and the cemetery paths are just grass and mud." He explained to Karen.

They turned down a little gravel road heading north until they came to a bend heading west. Hugh oak trees shaded the tombstones The little cemetery looked nice since it had recently been mowed. However, there were few flowers. A sign saying that flowers were forbidden explained why real flowers were absent but a few artificial flowers were in urns on the tombstones. Grandma placed day lilies from the farm in front of a large stone.

Grandma commented, "I know the sign reads 'no flowers,' but Alice loved flowers. They will be taken away after they die."

No one commented on that.

One side of the stone read – 'Joseph William Miller - May 14,1975.' The other side read – 'Alice Boender Miller - beloved wife and mother - born August 4, 1977 ; died February 24, 2002.'

"*August 4th is today,*" thought Karen. *It's appropriate that we come on my mother's birthday. She was 23 years old, the same age that I am. Dad was almost 27 years old when mom died.*

"*That is a coincidence. I wonder how many coincidences I can find? I wish that Jim could be here with me. His stone is in California with the name of James Wells on it. That's wrong. Everything is wrong. He was too young to have died in Afghanistan.*"

"*I wonder if Dad knows about Jim? I wonder where Dad is now? He would only be 49 years old. According to Grandma Rose,*

I have a half- sister, Grace Elizabeth Miller. She must be 17 - years - old now. I wonder if I find her, could I also find my father?"

The clouds covered the sky. Karen felt an eerie feeling that sent chills up her back. Suddenly it started to rain big warm drops. Everyone made a mad dash for the car.

As they drove past the corn fields, Grandma noticed the seven-foot-tall corn leaves that had curled from the high temperatures. "We need this rain," She remarked.

Then it stopped raining. The air was still. Even the birds were silent.

"Look behind us!!" Jack pointed to the dark, swirling funnel cloud coming from the northwest.

Ryan drove a half mile, but knew that the twister was faster than the car. He turned sharply into the nearest driveway, which happened to belong to his father's friend, John Mast.

They all scurried out of the car with Ryan helping his grandmother onto the porch. Jack pounded on the door while Karen rang the doorbell. Ryan opened the unlocked door of the house and yelled, "John, are you home? I'm Ryan Boender. Can we come in?"

A faint voice answered, "Come to the basement."

They hurried into the foyer and saw the steep, dim lit, stairway leading to the basement. Ryan and Jack saw that Grandma Rose could not manage the steep stairs without some help. John and his wife, Margie, were standing at the bottom of the stairs. The roar of the tornado was growing louder. Karen said, "Grandma Rose, turn sideways and take one step at a time while holding on to the hand rail. Ryan and Jack will be just below you. If you miss a step, they will catch you. I will be in front of you so I can grab you if you start to fall." They were relieved to reach the bottom of the stairs.

"Let's get into the next room," John ordered. "A tornado is coming." They passed a room with an open door that was under the stairs. Grandma saw the shelves full of jars of canned food and wistfully remembered her full basement shelves from five years ago.

"The cupboard is probably the safest room, but I'm not sure that we can all fit in it. Besides, if the tornado hits the house, we would get a lot of glass blown on us."

Ryan turned to their hosts and tried to introduce his cousin but his voice was lost in the roar of the tornado. It sounded like a train had just passed over the house.

Karen hugged her grandmother.

"Don't worry. The worst is over." Grandma Rose reassured her.

"I've been in an earthquake but never in a tornado," Karen said. "If there's an earthquake, you don't want to be in a building. I remember my dad, I mean Matt Wells, was sitting in a dentist chair in Mexico below Yuma, Arizona. I was in the waiting room. I ran outside. Soon, the dentist in his white uniform and my dad with a white bib on ran out and called my name. They were looking for me."

"Was everyone okay?" Ryan asked.

"It was only a five on the Richter scale so it didn't do much damage, except some glass was broken and pictures fell off the walls. The epicenter was in Mexicali on the border of California and Mexico."

The wind was still blowing but the sound of the tornado had calmed down. "I think the tornado has passed over us so we had better check the damage." John said.

Everyone went up the stairs ahead of Ryan who was helping his grandmother. At the top of the stairs, Ryan's cell phone rang. "Hi Ryan, are you okay?"

Ryan answered, "Yes." He put the phone on speaker mode.

George's voice was panicky. "I went to my mother's house and couldn't find her."

"Don't worry. She is with us. She is okay. Grandma, Karen, Jack and I took the car to go to the cemetery to see Karen's mother's grave. We saw the tornado in the distance and stopped by the John Mast house and went to the basement. We are all fine."

"I need help. Bessie's calf is up a tree."

"Did you say the calf is up a tree?" Ryan asked, not sure he has heard George correctly.

George answered, "Yes, she is about twelve feet up in the tree by the barn. The tornado just sucked her up and she landed in the tree."

Ryan queried, "What do you want me to do?"

"You have to climb the tree and drop the belt we used for the hogs and then the person below her has to fasten it around the calf's stomach. Then we will use pulleys and ropes, to get her down. Can't you hear Bessie bellowing and the calf crying?"

"Okay. We'll be there as soon as we can."

Ryan gave a weird laugh at the thought of a calf stranded in a tree. "You heard what my Dad said. Thank you so much for the shelter but we need to hurry home. I hope you don't have too much damage."

John said, "Thank God. Everyone is okay. From the window, it looks like we just have some tree limbs down. Go help that poor calf."

Chapter 8

Ryan drove slowly and carefully since there was debris on the road. They stopped twice to remove branches from Highway 5 on their way home to the Boender farm. Water covered the highway in two places but it appeared to be only a few inches deep. Ryan drove right through it splashing dirty water on the sides of the car.

No one spoke a word. In the back seat, Jack noticed that Karen took a deep breath. Apparently she knew the rule that you don't drive over a road if there is water across it. He reached over and held her cold hand. Karen didn't acknowledge the action. At least, she didn't pull away from him.

As he turned onto the graveled drive way, Ryan heard a loud sigh of relief from Grandma as she said, "Thank God, the houses appear undamaged." However, they saw more downed branches from the maple trees in the front yard.

As soon as they stopped, Ryan and Jack ran to the barn to help George get the calf down from the tree. The young men climbed the tree and using a sling, ropes and a pulley, they lowered the bellowing animal. When released, Bessie-the cow, gave a snort and both cow and calf joined the herd in the pasture.

Karen and Grandma Rose went into the big house by the back door. Betty was sitting in the darkened kitchen, slumped in a chair with her head on the table.

"Are you okay?" Grandma and Karen asked in unison.

"I went to look for you but you were missing. I got all wet." Ellen sobbed. "Then George came in from the barn and jabbered something about a calf up a tree. Then he said, 'You are no help'."

"How did I know you were all in the car going to the cemetery?"

"I don't know what to do. I can't wash breakfast dishes or vacuum the living room or make more coffee or work on lunch."

Karen and Grandma Rose looked at each other. "Why not?"

"There is no electricity!" Wailed Ellen.

As Grandma Rose and Karen looked around the kitchen, they saw that the hands on the clocks on the wall and stove were not changing. The light was off that usually was on in the kitchen. The television was off.

The men came stomping into the house. With a light hearted chuckle, George said, "Well that is a first time for me. I never got a calf out of a tree before."

He sobered up when he saw that Ellen was so upset. "What's wrong?" He questioned.

Ellen raised her voice and in a high tone she shrieked, "Can't you see that there is no electricity!!!

"Let's all sit by the table and talk about this." George stated.

"I'd better go home and see if everything is okay," Jack announced.

"Let us know if you need any help," George said.

"Okay." Jack tiptoed out the door and held it so it wouldn't slam. He didn't want to make more trouble but he wondered if Ellen would even notice.

"The first concern is food." George stated.

"We have plenty of food." Grandma said. "Since you hooked up my gas stove to propane, we can cook on it. The electric start won't work but I have matches."

"The generator works the milking machine and the milk cooler so that won't be a problem for a few days. We will be sure to use it while it is light outside so we won't need to use the flashlights and lanterns to see." He turned to Ryan. "Is your cell phone working?"

"No, the tower must be down. Do you think that a downed transformer is why we don't have electricity?"

"Probably, but don't use your cell phone just to chat with someone. We don't know how long the battery will last."

"But I can charge it with the car hook- up."

"I don't know how much gas is in the car and the pumps won't be running at the gas station without electricity."

"I thought that Ryan said you have both propane and fuel tanks outdoors." Karen inquired.

"Yes, but the fuel tank is diesel for the tractor." George explained.

Ryan laughed. "I can just see a string of neighbors running their tractors down the road on their way to get groceries. Maybe they could go 15 miles an hour."

"But the grocery stores and pharmacies would be closed since they can't run their electronic cash registers and lights without electricity." George explained.

"It's hot and going to be hotter tonight. How can I sleep without air conditioning?" This brought on a fresh crying jag from Ellen.

"Ellen, why don't you go to the camper and rest? I'll start the generator in the RV to bring you cool air. We even have solar panels on the camper but I don't know if they will run the air conditioner."

George continued, "Karen and mom, can you disconnect all appliances to prevent a surge of power once the power comes back on. Then you can make lunch but don't hold the refrigerator or freezer doors open any longer than necessary. . . .Ryan, let's go find everything we may need and put everything where we can find it easily."

That night, George went to the camper to sleep with his wife, Betty. Grandma Rose said, "I don't need electricity for an air conditioner. I'll just sleep in my own bed with the windows open.

"Good idea, Grandma. I'll just stay in my own room." Ryan said. The reality was if he slept in the camper, he was afraid that he would hear his mother cry and complain.

Chapter 9

When Ryan returned from Jack's place, Grandma Rose asked Ryan to drive her to her friend Esther's house to ask her about a trip to Cantril.

Esther said that she would be happy to meet Karen and drive them to Cantril, but she didn't know if there was enough gas in her Honda to make the trip.

Rose assured her that George would fill her car with gas that he had saved in cans for lawn mowing.

They hoped that the store would be open, there was a good chance it would be open since the Amish store was about fifty miles away. After leaving Moravia on Highway 5, they followed the Iowa Scenic Road signs around curves and up and down tall hills to East Highway 2 toward Bloomfield. Soon they were on the Mormon Trail which was a part of Highway 2. This highway was a two lane paved road with extra wide shoulders for the Amish horses and buggies. They saw the horse droppings before they spotted a horse and buggy. A woman, who wore the typical dress and cap of the Amish, was driving from the left side of the buggy's front seat. The second buggy was driven by a man with a beard but no mustache. He wore the broad brimmed hat above his shirt, pants and suspenders.

Karen reached behind the seat and grabbed her cell phone from her purse. You could hear her excitement as she programed the phone. "I'll take a photo with my phone. It should have a full battery."

"Hurry before we pass them." Rose suggested. "Most bishops tell their Amish people not to have their faces photographed. That's why I don't have many pictures of your family to show you."

The horse turned right on a gravel road so Karen was able to photograph both horse and buggy without the man's face.

"I wonder why one driver used the right side of the front seat and the other used the left," she said.

Esther answered. "When you use the horse's reins to drive, it doesn't matter where you sit."

On the right hand side of the road they saw an Amish store with wooden rocking chairs and other yard chairs plus toys in the front.

"I want to go inside and look around." Karen said.

The beautiful chairs were made from solid hardwood such as Red and White Oak, Cherry, Maple, and Walnut. Most seemed to have Shaker and Mission features but inside the store they had a sign that advertised custom made furniture. But the women found custom made furniture, made by hand by the Amish, to be very expensive.

Other home decorations and toys were made of wood. Karen spotted a beautiful walnut lazy - susan that she thought Ellen would like, but didn't want to carry it in her luggage when she flew home.

"Buy it now." Esther suggested. "I can send it to you when you are in California."

Karen answered, "Maybe I shouldn't buy it since solid wood things require trees. Ellen may not want to display it on her dining room table because she doesn't want to offend any tree huggers."

Esther asked, "What's a tree hugger?"

Karen answered, "Anyone who believes we have to preserve trees."

Rose stated, "Look, this paper says that one company wants to be sure that trees are replaced and forest landscapes are restored so they plant a tree with every order of furniture."

Karen said, "I'll buy the lazy - susan and have Grandma Rose keep it for me. I'll tell Ellen that I saw many beautiful wooden things that the Amish made and get her reaction. If she says that it is a good idea to use beautiful wooden things, I'll have you send it to me to give to her for Christmas."

Continuing on their journey, they saw many farms with cows, horses and sheep. The yards and gardens were carefully tended. They didn't see any weeds. It looked like every building had a fresh paint job. Amish clothes, hanging on the clothes-line, completed the scene.

A huge red store, with a barn and pond, was located just outside of Cantril. "This is the "Dutchman's Store.," announced Esther.

Karen was curious. "I thought we were going to an Amish store, not a Dutchman's store."

Esther answered, "The store was founded by the Zimmerman family. They are Amish. They moved from Lancaster County, PA. Many Amish people speak a German dialect called 'Pennsylvania Dutch,'so they decided to call the store 'Dutchman's Store'."

The store was huge! Inside they found row after row of bulk goods such as flour, sugar, beans, rice, dried potatoes, and even beef jerky.

Fresh vegetables were for sale along with prepared foods such as jams and jellies.

"Look at all the jams and jellies." Karen said, "There is Mrs. Miller's Homemade Blueberry Jam. I wonder, could it have been made by my relatives?"

Esther said, "Miller is a common name in the US as well as a common Amish name." She picked up a jar. "This is made in Fredericksburg, Ohio. I don't think it is made by a near relative of yours."

Every kitchen item you may want to use for cooking, baking, and canning was not far away.

Another section contained little plastic containers or plastic bags of every spice you could imagine. Esther explained, "The prices are great since you don't pay for expensive packaging. I especially like 'Farm Dust' seasoning for meats."

"What in the world is 'Farm Dust?' questioned Karen.

Esther handed the plastic container to Karen. She read the label. "It's a mixture of Himalayan salt, dried onion and garlic, black pepper, fennel, marjoram, thyme, rosemary, sage, oregano and basil. It can be used wherever you use salt and pepper but it's more flavorful."

They moved to another area of the store which had thousands of bolts of fabric in muted tones as well as darker material. Some bolts of fabric had flower prints. Bindings, needles and thread were nearby. Beautiful quilts were also for sale.

Readymade pants, suspenders, men's shirts, men's broad brimmed hats plus women's dresses and caps were for sale in every size. Children's clothing was a miniature of the adult clothing.

Grandma Rose decided to buy many bulk items such as flour, sugar, and dried potatoes and even beef jerky. She also needed spices to refurnish her kitchen. Since she didn't have a car or driver's license, she needed to rely on others to take her to the store.

Karen bought some candy from the bulk bins, but didn't buy much because she didn't want to take items on the plane. Esther bought several jams and of course Farm Dust.

"If you have everything, let's go home." Esther said. "I have peaches to can."

"Okay," Grandma Rose answered, "But please wait until I use the bathroom." She hoped that it was a modern facility with flush toilets and a handicapped bar. She soon found out that it was.

As they traveled home, Grandma Rose wondered out loud if the electricity would still be out.

"It's hard to tell since there are no traffic lights on Highway 2." Esther answered.

Grandma continued, "I should have bought those nice round candles with several wicks. The beeswax candles smell so good when the candle is burning."

Chapter 10

The electricity was restored by the time the women arrived back to the Boender home.

Ryan unloaded his grandmother's groceries and carried them into her little house. "I see why you wanted the storage space near the kitchen. What are you going to do with so much food?"

Rose laughed. "I'm going to give some of it to you. Try this beef jerky."

Ryan savored the salty meat taste. "Yes, that's good. I can snack on jerky whenever I want something to eat and don't want to go to the cafeteria."

Rose added, "You never know when the electricity will go out again, sometimes there doesn't have to be a storm. I can use the bulk items to cook enough food for the family for a long time. My stove won't have an electric start but since it runs on propane, I can use it till we run out of propane. I'll use matches to start it. Your dad can probably use the grill too."

"Mom will be grateful. She wouldn't know how to fix meals without the microwave."

"Fresh vegetables and fruit are healthy and next year we will have plenty of it when you help with the garden."

"Sure, Grandma Rose. I promise that I'll help you in the garden. I'll help you eat it, too, even if there isn't a blackout or food shortage."

The men had cleaned up the branches. Since few trees and branches had fallen on fences, it was a quick fix. Now they let the cows out of the barn to graze in the pasture before milking them.

- - - - - - - -

Karen had much to think about after the Cantril trip. She was fascinated by the Amish way of life. She sat down by Ann's desk in the bedroom and pondered her family history so she could write it down.

"Let's see. Grandma was brought up Amish and married a Dutchman named Peter Boender whose parents came from the Netherlands. They attended the Reformed Church in Pella. Peter bought a farm when he married Grandma Rose. Because there wasn't a Reformed Church nearby the farm, they attended the Methodist Church in Albia.

My mom, Alice Miller, became Amish when she married my father, Joseph Miller, from Moravia. I lived with my Aunt Ellen and Uncle Matthew Wells, and brother Jim, after my mother died. I was moved from rural Iowa to San Diego, California. Ellen and Matthew Wells never told me that I was born Karen Miller. They called me their daughter but they never adopted me. Ellen enrolled me in school and used the name of Wells as my last name.

"My father married again and had a daughter named Grace who is my half-sister. My brother, Jim, died in Afghanistan. I don't think he knew anything about Grandma Rose and Grandpa Peter. At least he never told me about it.

"Who am I? I need to try to find my father and half-sister, Grace. I want to learn more about my heritage but school is starting next week and I'm the teacher at Eisenhower Elementary in San Diego, California. Now I need to fly back to my apartment in San Diego.

"Maybe I can fly back here during Christmas break and learn more about my family and experience winter in Iowa."

Rose was invited to eat with the family, at the big house, since Grandma Rose had not fixed anything for supper.

Karen asked if Ryan could drive her back to the airport in Des Moines on Tuesday since school started next week.

"I need to go back to Ames for classes on Thursday so that will be fine," Ryan assured her.

"Will you be able to return to Iowa for Christmas?" he asked.

George spoke up. "You are welcome anytime."

Betty stammered, "But Ann will also be home then so it would be crowded."

Rose chimed in. "Of course she is welcome. If there isn't room at George's house she can stay with me and sleep on the sofa."

Karen answered, "Thanks for the invitation. It will be nice to meet my cousin Ann. . . . I'll check the internet and see what more I can learn about my family and heritage."

That evening Jack asked Karen to go on another walk with him, down by the creek. They sat down on a tree stump and talked. He had a tear in his eye as he said, "I know that Ryan and I have to go back to college and you need to go back to teaching but I will miss you. I hope we can keep in touch on Facebook and messages on the internet."

Karen responded, "Yes. I would like that."

Jack put his arm around Karen and pulled her into an embrace as he kissed her. She was surprised but did not object.

Chapter 11

The flight to San Diego was uneventful. Since there was a storm coming from the Pacific Ocean, the flight was mostly over Nebraska, Colorado, New Mexico, Arizona and into California. There was little turbulence, until they were close to the border of southern California. This gave Karen some undisturbed time to think about what she had experienced in Iowa, and how it affected her life. The plane landed all too soon at the airport.

Karen spent the next couple of days preparing for the fourth grade class she was going to teach this year. She knew she should phone her mother, but it was her mother who phoned her.

"Did you finally get the Iowans out of your system?" asked Ellen.

"Actually, I enjoyed my visit. I may even return to Iowa during the Christmas break."

Ellen coughed and sputtered, "You have got to be kidding! Jim won't be here so we will be alone." Matt, Ellen's husband, said nothing but had a pained expression on his face.

"Was my mother doing okay?" Ellen added more gently.

"Grandma Rose is doing well, but she has some problems ambulating."

Ellen added. "We never got along very well. We are too different. She has puritanical thoughts and is churchy. She never had more education than eighth grade. Does she still use expressions like 'hunky dory', or 'swell', or 'that's a fine kettle of fish?' Kids were 'knee high to a grasshopper'. If you repeated something, she said, 'You sound like a broken record.' "

Karen defended her grandmother. "Grandma Rose was very gracious to me. She is a wonderful cook and baker. . . . She reads and sews in her spare time."

In a sarcastic voice, Ellen added, "Do they all live in the little house that I was raised in? I bet it is still very provincial."

Karen answered. "Yes, they live in the same house on the farm, but it has new siding and a new roof. Betty had new cupboards, a new bathroom and all new appliances put into the house before she moved in three years ago. Grandma has her own tiny house on the property."

Ellen commented, "I didn't like Betty either. She is too ethnocentric, or I suppose narcissist is a better word. Everything in her world revolves around her. . . . Why don't your dad and I meet you for dinner at the Savory Shrimp place that your dad likes so well? Would Friday be good? No, Fridays are too crowded. How about Saturday evening at seven o clock?"

Karen answered. "Okay, Saturday is fine."

On Saturday, Karen arrived at the restaurant a few minutes before seven, but spotted her family right away. The Wells family was already seated. Ellen's coif appeared as if she had just come from the beauty shop. Her designer suit fitted her slim body perfectly. Matt wore khaki pants with a white shirt and brown jacket. Karen wore a knit shirt and jeans.

Ellen saw Karen looking for them. "Here we are. You are almost late. You can sit beside Matt."

Ellen began the conversation about her mother, Grandma Rose. "I bet your Grandmother Rose wears an apron everywhere, just like the Amish," she stated.

"No. Grandma Rose wears pockets in her apron and the Amish don't use pockets. She only wears an apron on the farm but it is always white. White aprons mean you are single and black,aprons mean you are married-"

"Don't be a smart ass!!" Matthew injected. "Respect your mother." He firmly stated.

The waiter arrived at the table for their drink and dinner orders, so nothing was said about the Iowa family for a few minutes.

Ellen interrupted the uneasy silence with a question. "Where did you go in Iowa? Everything is so far away from the farm. My longest vacation in Iowa was to go to the Iowa State Fair and see the huge hogs and the life size cow made of butter."

"We didn't go to the fair. We went to a wonderful Amish store in Cantril and to the grave sites of my parents. . . . I'd like to find my father if he is still alive."

Matthew's face became red as he blustered, "I am your father. The man that raises you is your father. I have given you clothes, toys, dancing lessons, a trumpet to play in band, vacations to the ocean, and even a college education. I am your father!"

"Yes, you gave me things. Thank you." Karen answered in a small voice. What she thought but didn't say out loud was, *"Yes, you are my father but what I wanted to say was I would like to meet the man who married my mother and gave me my DNA, which includes my genetic blueprint. I may even need this for health reasons. How much is heritage incorporated into your personality?"*

Little was said when the food arrived. Although the shrimp was perfectly prepared, Karen ate only a small amount.

"Is it okay if I get a take-out bag and enjoy some of this tomorrow?" Karen asked. She knew that her mother would never eat left-overs.

"Go ahead." Ellen said with a sigh.

Karen returned to her apartment and went to bed as soon as she had taken her shower. She wondered why it was so hard to visit with her parents. It felt like they didn't really approve of her. She had tried so hard to please them over the years. She still longed for her brother, Jim. He always kept the conversation going. They approved of everything he said and did.

Chapter 12

Karen ran up the stairs to her apartment after a hectic day of teaching fourth graders. Since she wasn't very hungry, she made a sandwich of the chicken salad she had bought from the deli. Turning to the desk, which was at the end of her kitchen cupboards, she dumped the homework assignment papers on top. She knew she should correct the papers on English grammar but wasn't in the mood.

Instead, Karen sat down at the desk and turned on her computer as she ate the sandwich. In the two weeks after Karen arrived at her home in San Diego, she had received nothing from her Iowa family, but today there was an email from Jack.

Dear Karen,

I miss your smiling face and our talks.

Have you learned more about your father and half-sister?

My classes are going well except for trigonometry. I don't know why the study of triangles has applications to farming, unless I get a job in county engineering.

I am taking a class in genetics because of our talks. Genetic testing of DNA on animals and people can show the likelihood of certain diseases and 'have insights in their health and wellbeing'. If you can't find out more about your birth mother and father, you may want genetic testing to find out more about yourself.

The weather here is great, with 75 degrees in the day and 50 degrees at night. We haven't had a frost yet, so the maple and oak leaves on campus have not turned red and gold. I'm looking forward to fall and even more to winter, when I get to see you during Christmas break.

Hope you are doing well.
Your friend,
Jack Welsh

Karen smiled at the email. Now what should she say to Jack? Her parents, Ellen and Matt, wanted her to be with them at Christmas in San Diego. The problem was that all they talked about was her brother, Jim. You would have thought he was a saint. The photos, high school football trophies, and a purple heart encased in a frame were sitting on the mantle of the living room as a shrine to him. Karen missed her brother, too, but it had been three years since he died.

Karen wanted Christmas to be a happy time.

There weren't any photos of her on the mantle of the fireplace. When she asked about it, Ellen said, "We are waiting for your wedding photo to put there."

Karen thought about what to answer Jack. She wanted to be friendly, but not too friendly, so she decided to answer his question about her father first.

Jack,
My efforts to locate my father aren't going very well, since he was or is Amish. Grandma and I went to the Monroe County Courthouse before I left Iowa. Jean Vander Veen, a church friend of Grandmother's, worked in the clerk's office. She said that she was not supposed to copy birth certificates except to the people on the certificate, but there wasn't any record of Joseph William Miller born on May 14, 1975. There wasn't any record of my birth either. Jean said that if we were born in an Amish home, and no one gave the county a notice of our births, they wouldn't have a record.

56

I can't find a social security number for my father either. That would be helpful since the record shows where you were born and when someone applied for it. Jean said that in 1965 the U.S. Congress allowed the Amish community to break from the Social Security system. In other words, they would no longer contribute to it. Of course, they wouldn't be eligible to collect money from it.

Dad was born in 1975, so no one had to sign for a number for him.

Since the Amish don't believe in being in the military, there isn't any military record either. The county records office doesn't have any record of him.

Of course, I need a social security number as a teacher. Ellen somehow got a social security number for me when I was a child. I think she used a fake adoption paper instead of a birth certificate.

School is going well but this fourth grade class is very restless, so I need to keep changing activities. They are very good in sports though. It's funny that some classes, as a group, are more energetic one year than another year.

Yes, I still plan to go to Iowa for Christmas. I want Christmas to be a happy time and Ellen and Matt are not very happy people. I look forward to seeing my grandmother and other family members. Yes, I look forward to seeing you too.

Your very good friend,
Karen

Dear Jack,
Today is November 29, the day after Thanksgiving.

Ellen served a wonderful traditional Thanksgiving dinner with turkey, mashed potatoes, green bean casserole and pies, but I don't know, or really care, how much of it she prepared. Matt's much younger brother was present with his wife, Shirley, and their four children.

After I helped with the clean – up, I played with the kids. Carter seemed lost, since his older brothers played together, and the baby was barely walking, so I played Sorry and Uno with him. He is very intelligent for a six – year – old. He reminds me somewhat of my brother, Jim, but there is no bloodline there. Maybe it is because Jim was my best playmate as a child.

Do you have much snow in Iowa? Will it be a dangerous drive from Ames to your parent's farm? One hundred and thirty miles is a long way to travel if the highway is icy.

When do you begin Christmas break? Our classes end on December 20, which is a Friday. I plan to fly to Des Moines on December 21. That makes it three weeks and one day until I see you, unless that won't work with your schedule.

Your very good friend,
Karen

Chapter 13

Karen waited and waited for an answer, but it was two weeks later that Jack finally wrote to her.

Dear Karen,

Have you found out more information about your father?

It's the first of November already. I look out the window and see that the leaves on campus are still the glorious colors of scarlet, orange, and yellow.

Pumpkins are everywhere. They are used as decorations for Halloween and Thanksgiving. I usually don't choose pumpkin pie, but I even ate it at the student café. It wasn't as good as I remember your grandma's pumpkin pie.

I love having four seasons a year. Don't you get tired of just sunshine? Okay, you get rain too.

I sit by my desk, in the dorm room that I share with John, and try to study, but all I think about is you. I want to tell you how I feel about you, but don't want to scare you.

I should be studying Statistics, but all I think of is you. Have you ever seen forests of trees in brilliant color? What are you doing? Do you think of me? You are still coming to Iowa during for Christmas, aren't you?

Please say that you are looking forward to coming to Iowa and seeing me. I want you to experience an Iowa Christmas.

Didn't you say that you had Dutch in your heritage, too? Pella isn't too far away and always plans the Pella Tulip Festival the first weekend in May. I hope that you will come for spring break too. Pella parades are the best since they have two corporations who create beautiful and or funny floats.

You can stay at your grandmother's house or you can come to my parent's house. I want you to meet my parents. I want them to know about the wonderful girl, no woman, that I met.

John, my roommate, says that I must be in love. Is it too soon to say that I love you? What do you think? I hate that you are so far away. I want you to be by my side forever.

Love,
Jack

Karen wrote three emails, but deleted them one by one, before she answered the last one.

Dear Jack,
Please don't be angry with me. Let me tell you how I feel. You are a very good friend, but I'm uncomfortable with promising more than that. I want to be your good friend, but please, let's not push it. I don't want to make plans for the future except to say that I am looking forward to seeing you at Christmas.

You are a very good friend, but let's take this friendship a little slower. Maybe our relationship will last and lead to marriage. It's too soon to tell, but I believe marriage should be "till death do us part." I'm not ready to think about it. You don't really know me. I don't even know myself very well.

Thanks for keeping in touch.
Karen

Dear Karen,
Okay, I will be careful to be patient with you, and try to keep our relationship as good friends. I don't want to lose you by being too romantic.

I have been interested in genetics. It's the old story of nature versus nurture. Is it possible to inherit genes that indicate you are musically inclined? How about sports? Do you like sports because your body is tall or robust? Or, do you like music and sports because your parents are interested in them and encouraged them?

Then I thought about the word Grace. To me, Grace is graceful. It is a beautiful movement as in a dance. I looked up the definition in three dictionaries. I received such diverse answers as: to give beauty to - quality of being — act of kindness — displaying grace in form or action; pleasing in appearance. Another meaning is **"The unmerited divine assistance given to a person."** *Your Grandmother Rose would like that.*

You are all of these. I'm sure that your half - sister is beautiful and charming and graceful, just like you. How could she help it, since she is your sister?

I'm waiting for your reply. Please email me. I miss you so much!
Love,
Jack

Dear Jack,
No, I don't have any more information about my birth father. I asked Grandma Rose, "Who bought the cemetery stone with my parent's dates on it." She answered, "Pete and I did. Since I couldn't be at the funeral, because of the car accident, I wanted a place where I could go to remember Alice. I wanted people to remember her, and know that she was married and was a good mother. I had them write 'beloved wife and mother' on it. Most tombstones have both husband and wife written on them, so I decided to add Joe's name. I don't remember who said his birth date was May 14, 1977."

Grandma didn't even know where he was born.
Thanks for keeping in touch,
Your friend,
Karen

Chapter 14

J ack's answer to Karen sounded like a recital of possible jobs
he could have with a degree in agriculture, although most
of them required further education.

Dear Karen,
Okay, I will behave myself and not tell you the romantic
things that I feel.
I don't want you to forget this young farmer, who will prob-
ably never be able to support a family on just 50 acres of land. Of
course, there are other jobs in agriculture with a person who has a
degree in agriculture. I'm not sure what specialty I want.
Environmental specialists study the impact of various human
actions on the environment. They recommend various solutions to
environmental issues. You can work in power plants or chemical
plants to find more efficient ways of disposing hazardous materials
that help to limit an impact on the environment.
Agricultural journalists work for various media outlets and
report on events and stories that are relevant to those working in
the agricultural field. They may report the weather conditions
for farmers, too.
A park manager performs all operations involved in managing
a park. These include supervising the park's development, main-
taining its facilities, overseeing the work of employees and volun-

teers. They plan conservation of the park's natural resources, hiring personnel, and managing budgets.

A park ranger needs to know the laws in his assigned area with regards to wildlife. He works with wildlife biologists who study animals in their natural habitat and observe their behavior, preferred habitats and biology. They see how human behavior and actions have an impact on animal habitats. They also observe ways that diseases are spread among animals. They spend much time in the wild and then study the results in the laboratory.

Agronomists mainly deal with the health and well-being of crops, with the purpose of increasing their overall production and efficiency. Research is usually done by others, while agronomists use their acquired knowledge and then recommend various solutions to farmers.

Of course, agricultural veterinarians usually work with farmers and ranchers and make sure that their animals are healthy and fertile. Their job duties include vaccinating the animals against diseases and treating various injuries and illnesses. They may also assist with the birthing of farm animals too.

Another job is to become an Agriculture science teacher to educate high school students on issues regarding agriculture, nutrition and natural conservation. They can also provide students with information, through FFA and 4-H, to prepare them for agriculture-related jobs.

See, I can write to you about issues that matter to me, without including references of my feelings for you.

Your undecided friend,

Jack

- - - - -

Karen sent her next email a couple of days later.

Dear Jack,

I'm glad that you are okay with my last email. I don't want to hurt your feelings.

Thanks for the photo of Ryan, you and me. I put it on my desk at home so you are always near me. Do you really think that I will forget you?

My friend, Marcia, came over to visit and asked, "Who are those cute guys?" I answered, "They are my first cousin and his friend, although it seems like Ryan should be a closer relative than a cousin, since we both have the same Grandmother and think amazingly alike."

I am going to Ellen and Matt's house for Thanksgiving dinner, since I won't be with them for Christmas. I think of them as Ellen and Matt, instead of Mom and Dad, now that I know they aren't my birth parents. Who are your real parents? The people who raised you, even though your personalities are so different, or your genetic parents? Are musical and sport traits inherited or the result of your environment? Grandma Rose said that I remind her so much of her daughter, Alice. She also said that I look very much like Alice. In the one photo that Grandmother took when I was a baby, I don't think I look like Alice. She was more beautiful with her long, curly hair and dark brown eyes, but I guess it is true that 'beauty is in the eye of the beholder.'

I need to grade more fourth grade papers. It seems like I am always grading papers, but I try not to get too far behind.

Your very good friend,
Karen

Chapter 15

Dear Jack,
 The children are getting excited about Christmas. We are not allowed to put Christ in Christmas in the class room, or for their party for themselves and their parents. The kids sing: "Jingle Bells, Oh Christmas Tree, Rudolf the Red Nosed Reindeer, and Frosty the Snowman." They didn't understand why Frosty melted, since they haven't seen snow melt.

One day when they were very energetic, I decided to sing, "I Saw Mommy Kissing Santa Claus," which was a song that made me laugh as a kid. They were quiet as they listened to me. They liked it and laughed too.

I am looking forward to a Christmas with snow. Do you still ride a sled down the hill between your farm and the Boender Farm? Ryan said that it was a good sledding hill. I want to try it once. Some of my friends have gone to the mountains to ski, but I never have.

Tomorrow I will pack my warmest clothes to fly to see my relatives and you. Will it be a problem to pick me up from the Des Moines airport on Saturday, December 21?

Looking forward to seeing you and having an Iowa Christmas.
Karen

Dear Karen,
I'm so looking forward to seeing you on the 21ˢᵗ of December. I know that Ryan will let me go with him to get you from the air-

port. He won't be my friend anymore if he won't let me see you as soon as possible. Just kidding.
Jack

When Karen landed at the Des Moines airport twenty minutes early, she wondered how long she would have to wait for Ryan and Jack to find her and give her a ride to the Boender farm. She hurried to the rest room and then to the baggage area to find her suitcase with the purple ribbon on the handle.

She bent over to pick up her suitcase when she heard a familiar voice yelling, "THERE SHE IS!"

Jack ran to her and gave her a big hug. She turned to Ryan and hugged him and wondered if the pretty young woman in a blond ponytail beside him was a new girlfriend. Ryan kept his arm around her and said, "This is my sister, Ann. She didn't want to wait at home to meet you."

"Hi, cousin Ann. Do you want a hug too?"

Ann shyly hugged Karen.

"Let's get this show on the road," Jack said. "We have a lot to do yet today."

Karen gazed at the snow covered houses. Although the road was cleared of snow, everywhere else appeared white. Karen saw the fields and forests they passed, which looked like a white wonderland similar to what she had seen on Christmas cards.

Ryan and Jack chatted about the big evergreen tree they were going to cut down. "You could come with us and chop the last bit of tree." Jack said. Ryan added, "Then we will be able to decorate it tonight."

Karen said, "I don't think that I can go with you; I don't have any boots to wear."

Ann responded, "Either my mother, Grandma, or I can find you some boots. Mom and I wear the same size. You can wear mine and I will wear Moms. That will sit better with my mother. I have extra coats and gloves that you can borrow, too."

Karen thanked Ann. Clearly, Ann and her mother didn't have the same personalities. Ann was thoughtful of others, while Betty thought about herself first.

The snow started falling again around Knoxville, but Ryan drove carefully. He was used to driving in the snow.

Ann told Karen that Albia Trinity Church was having a choir concert for the service in the morning. "We don't want to miss that. They have been practicing for months, and are really good."

Karen said, "I'd like that. . . .If I may borrow some of your old outdoor clothes, I want to slide down the hill between your family farm and Jack's place."

Ryan answered, "We'll use the toboggan." Jack's thoughts were that he would sit behind Karen and hold on to her as they slid down the hill.

Before going to the main house, Karen wanted to see Grandma Rose. Grandma saw them coming down the driveway and opened her front door, with a giant size smile on her face. She was so happy to see Karen and Ann.

Ryan explained that since Ann was home, she would sleep in her own bed. Of course, Karen could sleep on the sofa in Grandma Rose's house. Grandma turned to Ryan and asked, "Ryan, will you bring Karen's suitcase in here?"

Before losing the late afternoon light, they hiked a half - mile up the hill to where the Douglas Fir trees were growing. Ryan pulled the toboggan they would use to carry the tree home.

Karen was awe struck at the beauty of the covered forest. She had never before seen tiny tracks in the snow from the animals and birds that lived in the forest.

Ann suggested that they find a little tree for Grandma Rose.

Jack and Ryan had no problem loading the trees onto the toboggan.

Karen had not expected the forest to become so enchanting. Afternoon light and shadows had turned the snow into a soft glow. Then it was sunset and the red and yellow from the setting sun filled the sky. She wanted to stay in the forest until the full moon rose, but knowing she had to go with the others, she took a long look at the forest and caught up with the others. She turned around and looked behind her before they entered the house and saw the moon rise. The stars seemed so close that it felt like you could reach up and touch them. Karen was in awe because in San Diego, the lights interfered with star gazing.

They hurried home to decorate both trees. Grandma Rose told them where to hang the ornaments because she couldn't reach very far to hang them. Betty changed a few bulbs 'to make it more centered' but, for the most part, allowed the young people to decorate it as they wished.

Ellen said that Karen "wouldn't do it right," so Karen never got the pleasure of decorating a tree as a child. Ellen had her own ideas about her artificial tree that had to be decorated in Ellen's style.

When they went to the barn to milk cows, George came to Ryan and said, "Come over in the back of the barn and see what I bought." Ryan followed his father to the back of the barn while George explained, "This really isn't a Christmas gift, but I thought we could fix it up during your Spring break."

Ryan saw what looked like a truck under the tarp. He eagerly lifted the tarp which covered a blue and white Ford 100 pick-up truck. Ryan saw that it was clearly a very old model because of the square front end.

"It looks very old," Ryan commented trying not to show his disappointment.

George's smiling face showed his happiness over his purchase. "I recently bought this old truck from my golfing friend, Mark. He inherited it after his father died. They were planning to put it in the farm auction unless I bought it first. It's a 1978 diesel model. I checked with my other golfing partner, David, to see if his friend from Raleigh could check it out as a possible vehicle that would work after an EMP or solar pulse. He said it would be a good one because it doesn't have all those electronic parts."

George continued, "We can always use another pick-up. I'm glad that it is a diesel truck because we have a large diesel storage tank for our tractors. Since farm diesel is dyed red, we can't normally use that fuel on the road, but we will buy our diesel from the fuel station. If there is an EMP or solar pulse, no one will check us."

"But there is a pump on our storage tank." Ryan protested.

"I'm sure that we can convert it to gravity flow," his father stated.

"You are really taking this problem of an EMP or solar pulse very seriously, aren't you?"

"I guess I am," his father replied.

Chapter 16

Ryan and his father, George, returned to the barn. The cows needed to be milked and fed twice a day. They didn't know it was Christmas Day.

George was jovial as he said, "Look at that truck."

Ryan looked at the old pickup truck and wondered whether the Ford was in running condition.

"The engine is good and we can fix anything else when we work on it during Spring Break. We can always use another pick-up.

I'm also looking for a Volkswagen Beetle for Ann. It has to be made before 1975, since a Bosch fuel injector was added after that date."

Ryan knew then how seriously his father was taking the thought of going without electricity. He wondered if Ann would appreciate a very old car, but he didn't say anything about it. Instead he said, "Let's get on with the milking."

- - - - - - - -

The next day Jack arrived for a visit.

Jack smiled at Karen as he said, "I met a woman, well, a girl actually."

Karen had a funny feeling in her stomach. *Was she jealous?*

Jack laughed. "You should see the look on your face. Do you think that I have another girlfriend besides you? You are the one for me."

"Who is she and where did you meet her?" Karen asked.

"Her name is Martha Miller. I met her at a friend's Christmas party." Jack answered. "She is Amish, but is on her Rumspringa time so she must be at least 16 years-old."

"She is Amish, 16, and allowed to go to parties?" Karen questioned.

"Yes, Rumspringa means running around. The Amish allow their young people to mingle with us Englishers to be sure that they want to join the Amish in their faith. She hasn't joined the Amish church yet."

"What did you talk about?"

"You."

"I told her that I had a girlfriend whose father was Joseph William Miller. She also has a half-sister named Grace Elizabeth Miller. My friend, Karen Wells, is trying to find them."

Martha asked, "Is Karen Amish?"

Ryan answered. "No, but her birth father and mother were when they were married."

"What is her mother's name and where is she?" Martha queried.

"Her name was Alice Boender Miller, but she died when Karen was born. Since you are also a Miller, I wondered if you had ever heard about them?"

Martha answered, "I don't remember, but I can ask my mam and my aunt about them. Maybe they will know something about the family."

Jack then told her about the fact that Joe had remarried a woman called Katie. She had returned to Chicago and had a baby girl named Grace Elizabeth Miller. "She divorced Joe."

"Then he probably isn't Amish anymore since we can't get divorced. . . .How can I contact you if I find out anything?"

"I'll be back at college next week, but I can you give you my phone number and address in Ames. Will you use a phone or write a letter?"

"Yah, I will write to you or call you on the phone."

Chapter 17

Karen looked at the landscape as she traveled to the airport, in Des Moines, on her return trip home. The sky was grey, with storm clouds appearing above the brown and black countryside. The trees were black and reminded her of skeletons.

She was happy there wasn't much turbulence, from the storm, on her trip to San Diego. From the air, she viewed green palm trees and grass.

After she arrived to her apartment, she called Ryan to report that she had safely arrived home.

Ryan said that he would notify the family of her safe arrival, but the news caster was predicting a severe storm on the way to Iowa.

On January 9, a blizzard hit Iowa. The temperature was -17 degrees. The snow was two feet thick, where it wasn't drifting. It was the worst storm to hit Iowa since 1973.

Since Ryan had not left for college, after Christmas break; he drove the diesel tractor from the barn to the end of the driveway to clear an area to get to the barn. His plan was to go down the hill to break the ice on the pond so the heifers, calves, and the bull could get water. He needed to deliver a one - ton bale of hay, too.

Since the wind had blown onto the trail, it was smooth with the snow and it was difficult to tell where the trail meandered.

He slid into the invisible ditch! He went back and forth a few inches but he couldn't budge it. He walked home.

Then he called Jack but Jack had problems of his own. Their furnace didn't work. The electric heaters only got the temperature to 58 degrees in the house.

Jack layered his long underwear with two pair of pants, a flannel shirt, two coats, two pair of socks, farm boots and gloves. Jack's mother tied a wool scarf around his neck and face since it was difficult to tie the scarf on without taking off his gloves. He wore so many clothes that he could hardly walk to the barn for the tractor.

Then Jack had trouble getting his diesel tractor started. He pulled on the choke a few times. Finally, the tractor started. Now he had to drive the half mile to the Boenders with the wind whipping around him but he was so glad that the tractor had a cab around the driver.

The trees looked like filigree had covered them. The fields glistened with the sun shining on the snowbanks but Jack was glad that Karen had already left for California. This extreme cold weather may decide for her that she never wanted to live in Iowa.

At the Boenders, he waited for Ryan to add clothes before they took off on Jack's tractor to pull the Boender tractor out of the ditch. They stopped at the barn where Ryan added another shovel and a bag of sand which they tossed on the tractor floor. They drove down the trail until they saw the stuck tractor. Jack jumped down and added the rope between the two tractors. Ryan went to his tractor to steer it. Then Jack drove back and forth until both tractors were on the trail. After the ice was broken, they returned to Grandma Rose's house. She always had hot soup cooking in the fireplace. There they warmed up with soup and hot chocolate.

They warmed their hands, and the suction pieces of the milk machine, before they milked the cows. They were glad that the electricity was working.

Ryan picked up some tools and rode with Jack to his house. Again they were glad that they had a cab on the tractor since the wind was still blowing from the south west. Together they figured out that there wasn't any air intake to the outdoor furnace. The wind had blown the light snow into the regulator where it froze. They cleaned out the ice and snow.

Now the furnace worked.

Before Jack drove Ryan home on the tractor; they went to the Welsh chicken coop to feed the chickens corn, chicken feed, and fill the water containers with water. Jack's mom was glad that they gathered the eggs for her.

Chapter 18

Grandma removed the old coffee filter and dropped the grounds in a plastic jar that used to hold mixed nuts. She planned to put the lid on after the grounds dried. Then she would add the grounds to the manure that had not been inside a cow for three years. George planned to add that pile, from behind the barn, to the others to spread on the hay field, but saved it for his mother because of her request. She claimed that old manure did not smell as bad as fresh manure. Mixed with coffee grounds, the stuff made an excellent soil enhancer for her garden. She refilled the coffee maker with filtered water and added fresh coffee grounds to the pot. She lit the stove with her wooden matches. The coffee percolator started gurgling and spewing inside the glass bubble on the lid. The smell was delicious.

Grandma then wrote a note and put it on the refrigerator door with magnets to remind herself to buy coffee the next time she went to a grocery store. She smiled at the thought that George would want her to buy two of everything, so she would have extra in the event of a disaster.

It would be a good thing to go with Esther to the Amish store in Cantril and buy some of the Amish goods, but she needed to know what to buy.

George surprised her the next morning. "I can't do much in the field, since it has rained for two days. Let's take a little trip to the home of my friend, Richard Vos. He takes home-steading seriously."

George and his mother drove five miles to the Richard Vos homestead. Richard was in the driveway on his tractor, which pulled a small wagon filled with barrels of water he had hauled from the creek to his house. He didn't forgo modern equipment, but he didn't use electricity. Since his solar power was only good on sunny days, he wasn't working inside the house or machine shop on this cloudy day.

"Water is the most important resource on your homestead." Richard explained. "It is needed for your animals and plants, as well as your body." He showed them his hand-operated water pump that was hooked up to his well and piped to his house. "I also have a large water reservoir near my chickens and goats that uses creek water and provides water for our garden. We use the well water for our own use, but it is a shallow well, so we use it sparingly."

Richard showed them his rhubarb patch. He pointed to a patch of ground. "Over there, you will soon see the elderber-ries, and comfreys grow. The normal garden produce such as corn, beans, tomatoes, peppers, cabbage, and cucumbers will go over there but they are still growing in the hoop house.

"My wife makes jelly and cans what produce we don't eat as fresh vegetables and fruit." He pointed to his three apple trees. "Besides making applesauce and pies, she puts some in a large glass jar with water and sugar and then lets it ferment for four weeks until it is apple vinegar. Do you want to see my hoop house?"

Both George and his mother looked at him and asked, "Hoop house?"

"Well, some people call it a greenhouse, but a greenhouse is built with more permanent materials."

"Yes," they answered at the same time. The structure was shaped like a traditional greenhouse, but instead of glass, it had a heavy plastic covering. Both ends had doors large enough to drive a tractor through it. The plastic sides had rollers that could be rolled up to let the sunshine or breeze inside. Three raised beds, of black soil, were in a black tray, held up by wooden boards, which were about four feet off the floor. Small plants were growing from the shallow tray.

Richard was proud of his fourteen bee hives. "They not only pollinate the plants and trees but provide honey. You know that honey can be used to sweeten almost everything, and it won't spoil. If it becomes too thick to use, you only have to set the bottle of honey in warm water.

"We are careful to save enough energy from the solar power to run our small freezer, where we keep the meat from the beef that we buy when Dennis Sprick butchers his Angus heifer. If you want to homestead, you have to think about how your grandparents lived and not like the technology your grandkids use. In the event of a disaster that eliminates your electricity, your grandkids may not survive."

George and Grandma Rose said good-bye to Richard and his wife and went to the Chevy. George opened the front passenger car door for his mother and helped her into the car. He smiled as he said, "Now we are going to Cantril to the Amish store.

"I want to check the tools they have for sale and check the prices against Farm and Fleet prices. We have a variety of hammers, screw drivers, saws, pliers and files but I want to check their inventory. I also have most of what we need outdoors including shovels, pitchforks, hoes and rakes, but I want to price new fencing, too. You can help me choose tools for inside the house, such as for cooking and light."

Grandma Rose sighed and answered, "I always wanted some cast iron pans and a Dutch oven, but they are expensive."

George answered. "Good idea. We may have to do some cooking outdoors over a campfire. Cast iron pans are almost indestructible. Betty won't complain about her fancy cookware getting black, either. What else do you need inside the house?"

Grandma Rose answered, "Light is a problem. Candles are nice and smell good, but a couple of oil lamps will last longer and give more light. I would also like a new brush and tongs for my fireplace. Will you get some metal rigs to elevate my pots and pans? The metal grate that I have could also be replaced with a heavier one to allow more control of the heat when I'm cooking in the fireplace.

"Will it be okay if I buy some flour and sugar, since they sell it in bulk?"

George answered. "Buy any food you like."

George's mother looked directly into his eyes and said, "My social security check hasn't arrived yet. Will you pay for it? "

"Yes. I'll do it for you." In a teasing voice he added, "I will only do it if you will let me eat some of the cakes, cookies and breads you make."

Grandma laughed.

On the drive home, Grandma Rose thought about what Richard had said, "If you *want to homestead, you have to think about how your grandparents lived and not like the technology your grandkids use. In the event of a disaster that eliminates your electricity, your grandkids may not survive.*"

Chapter 19

Esther and her friend, Rose, rode to the church where the Women's Sparkle meeting was being held. The topic for this meeting was to plan for the semi - annual meeting when the community's other church women joined them for a luncheon and program.

They repeated their mission: The meaning of SPARKLE is:

S is for sharing.

P is for praying.

A is for action to help others.

R is for research,

And doing it all with Kindness,

Love, and Encouragement.

Connie, the president spoke, "Does anyone have a topic or speaker they want for the meeting?"

Everyone looked at the woman beside her. No one spoke. They knew if they spoke up, they would automatically be in charge of the program.

After a pregnant pause, Beverly said, "Ruth, since this is an election year, could you speak on something historical or political?"

There were a few soft groans. No one wanted anyone to know who was complaining.

Ruth answered, "I don't think politics is a good topic for this group. . . . I'd rather talk about being prepared for disaster from a Christian point of view."

"Are there any objections?" The president asked.

No one spoke.

"That's fine." The president said. "But will you do it?"

"Yes," answered Ruth.

Then Ruth thought, *What did I get myself into?*

Usually a talk like this was best if people could look at something, so she decided to do a show and tell.

Esther went with Ruth to Ottumwa, to Walmart, to look for a container. The best one they found was a medium - sized plastic container intended to be used to store dog food. It had a seal on it to prevent moisture or bugs from getting in.

She began her talk with the statement that people have lived for generations without electricity, but, today, most people don't know how to live without it. Being prepared for any disaster is to have food and water on hand.

A woman in a red dress raised her hand and asked, "Should we hoard food or just believe that God will take care of us?"

Ruth swallowed. "I believe that God wants us to help ourselves. The Bible gives us information about this. Mary, will you go to Proverbs 6:6-8 and read it for us?"

Mary stood up. She opened her Easy English Bible and read, "Lazy people should learn a lesson from the way that ants live. They have no leader or ruler, but they prepare their food during the summer. They get their food during the summer. They get it at the time of harvest to prepare for winter."

Mary sat down.

Ruth continued, "Remember that God also instructed Noah in Genesis chapter 6:13 - 21 to gather food for his family and grain for the animals. Joseph was told to gather food and grain during the seven good years to offset the seven years of famine in Genesis chapter 41.

"I'm writing about preparing for disasters and would like your input into what kinds of things we should store? Please pass out the papers and pens and write your list. What would you want to have in your house if all electricity was off and it might be weeks, months, or even a year before it was restored. You don't have to write your name on the paper, but I want to see your answers.

"I don't know when the world will end, or if Jesus will return in our lifetime. When you read Revelations, you do not read of the United States of America unless you feel that the Great Babylon mentioned is the USA. Remember Babylon was destroyed.

"The important thing to remember is - Are we preparing out of fear or because we want to feed our families and help others?"

Ruth pulled things out of her plastic box. First there was a hand can opener. "These are some of the things you will want to remember." She said. Then she pulled out cans of tuna, beans, soup and chili. Dry foods included raisins, cranberries and potatoes. Cereals were added. There was soap, because "You don't want to make it from ashes and pig fat."

The women laughed. Flashlights and batteries, candles and matches came out next. Seeds for next year's gardens were pulled out. "There are many more things you may want to add." Ruth said, as she pulled out the last two things from her box. They were baby wipes and toilet paper.

Now was the time for group discussion. Joan said that she lived in an RV for several years. "Most of the time we stayed in campgrounds but we also boondocked a lot. We had power from our batteries for lights. Our freezer, stove and refrigerator were powered by propane. Currently, we have empty tanks for both black and gray water. We also have a fresh water tank, but I don't know if there is fresh water in the tank.

"I suppose we would have to use our creeks and ponds, Lake Red Rock and Lake Rathburn and the Des Moines River for water. The problem would be that these sources may be contaminated and not safe to drink. Then the water would have to be screened, boiled, and bleach added to make it safe."

Ruth read from the lists the women had given her. Almost all of them wrote toilet paper.

They were remembering how scarce it was when Covid 19 happened. Connie's list added toothbrush, baking soda, games and books. Linda wanted instant coffee, grill, gas or wood for fires, fishing gear and kettles for cooking.

A couple of women wrote that they wanted a cave. There were many coal mines in Monroe County. Marion County had over 500 coal mines at one time, but all have been reclaimed. Would it be possible to dig into the side of hills to reopen some of them? You can see in the ditches where there are still seams of coal. Even though it was loaded with sulfur, perhaps it would still be fuel to burn. Maybe, the mines could also provide a place to store food or become a shelter.

One woman wrote the most poignant item. "I don't want to be alone."

Chapter 20

*D*ear Karen,
    I know that you are interested in history, especially your family's history. Since your grandfather was Dutch, you are also part Dutch. You would really like to visit the Pella area.

Many old buildings and shops have been built in the old Dutch style with typical three stories. Others dating from the early 1900's have been restored in Pella around the Garden Square.

Dutchmen, from the Netherlands, built the 125 foot working VerMeer Windmill to replicate a 1850 windmill from their country. On Franklin St., beside the museum, Dutch style buildings such as a church and bakery with many houses were moved into the area and restored to create a Dutch Museum and Village.

The best time to visit it is during Tulip Time the first weekend in May but many of the unique features of the town such as the Dutch Village, that I just described, can also be seen mid-March through December.

I will tell you first about the Tulip Festival. Over 800 people arrived from the Netherlands in 1847 because they were not allowed to worship as Reformists. During the Tulip Festival the Dutch people wear outfits similar to those worn in 1847. (They look similar to the Amish dress except the women have different hats and the dresses are more colorful. Although the men also have dif-

ferent hats, they wear clothes that an Amish man could wear such as homemade shirts and pants with drop seats or barn door bottoms.)

Before the parade these thousands of people, in their Dutch clothing, take mops and buckets of water and wash the streets. A few men will wear a yoke around their neck so they can carry two buckets. The kids like to run and splash each other as they push the mops down the street.

The floats are spectacular, especially those made by the two large corporations, Pella Corp and Ver Meer Manufacturing and Central College. Many more floats are made, especially by the church groups.

Sinterklaas, the Dutch Santa Claus, arrives on a white horse.

The local bands are quite good as they march down Franklin Street. A couple of years ago, the Pella band was asked to play in the Rose Bowl Parade.

Of course there are colorful tulips everywhere.

Is there any chance that you can come to Iowa the first weekend of May?

Hoping to see you soon,
Your best friend,
Jack

Dear Jack,
Pella sounds like a place that I want to visit.

I may come earlier, during Spring break, but not the first week in May. I have promised a teacher friend that I will help her to organize the decorating committee and help them decorate for their prom.

Now I need to correct my student's papers and plan next week's lesson plans.

Your friend,
Karen

Chapter 21

*D*earest Karen,
    I have the most wonderful news. Do you remember the Amish girl that I met at the party? Her last name was Miller. I told her about your search for your father. She didn't remember anything about Joe Miller, but promised to ask her mother and Aunt Mary about it. She sent me a letter at college that said that the Aunt Mary, not only knew Joe Miller, but Joe is her younger brother. An important looking letter was received at the Moravia Post Office for Joe Miller from Katie Miller. It also had a lawyer's name on it. Mary, and her mother, kept it and wanted to give it to Joe but he had already left. Neither Mary, or her mother, has never seen him again. The letter was post-marked in Oak Park, which is near Chicago. Mary's mother kept it with her important papers, but Joe Miller never came back to Moravia.

    The Amish girl is excited to meet you, since she feels you are her cousin. Her aunt, Mary Miller, will talk to Grandma Rose. If Grandma Rose verifies that you are Joe's daughter, the letter will be mailed to you. I have your Facebook and email addresses, but I need the address at your apartment.

    I have talked to Ryan about this. We will phone Grandma Rose tonight, but I think that you need to talk to her too. Grandma Rose will be the one who sends you the letter with the information.

Your very good friend,
Jack

Dear Jack,
Thank you! Thank you! Thank you! My address at my apartment is
3677 Park Blvd., San Diego, California 92103
Now I need to phone my grandmother and talk to her
about the letter.
Your best woman friend,
Karen

On the phone with Karen, Grandma admitted that she knew that Joe had left for Oak Park after Joe told his Grandmother, that Katie had phoned him. Katie said that she wasn't coming back to the farm. When neither George or Rose heard from Joe, George had gone to the Oak Park address and asked to see Joe. Katie's parents' housekeeper, Henrietta Jones, explained to George that she had answered the door and invited Joe into the foyer. Katie's mother came to the entry. Taking one look at Joe in a beard, and dressed like an Amish man wearing suspenders, Katie's mother, Elizabeth Van Wyk, said that they never knew anyone named Joe Miller. She slammed the door in his face. Elizabeth told the housekeeper that Joe must be Katie's husband; but never to invite Joe or George into the house or even tell Katie that he came for her.

The housekeeper didn't think that this was right, but she needed her job so she didn't tell anyone. One day, while cleaning Katie's room, she found an Iowa phone number. Henrietta copied the number on a slip of paper and put it in her apron pocket. After Grace was born she used the number to call Grandma Rose to tell her about the baby.

No, Grandma Rose didn't have the phone number, that Henrietta used, when she called Rose.

George told his mother that he was treated the same as Joe had been, and to leave the Van Wyk's alone. He didn't want to cause any trouble.

Karen then gave Grandma Rose her San Diego address.

Grandma Rose called Karen the next day, to tell Karen that she had a visit from Mary Miller. After Rose told Mary that Karen was Joe's daughter; the spinster sister of Joe Miller was happy to give Grandma Rose the registered letter, so it could be mailed to Karen.

"Be sure to let me know if you find out where Joe is living," Mary said. Grandma agreed. Then she put the registered letter in a large envelope and gave it to Esther to mail.

Karen waited three long days before the letter arrived. She tore open the envelope to find a sealed letter inside. It read, "This letter is to inform you that Katherine Ann Van Dyk Miller of 2020 Madison St, Oak Park, IL 60302 has petitioned the court to grant her a divorce from Joseph William Miller. She further states that she is to retain the property in Illinois and Joseph William Miller is to retain the property in Iowa. Furthermore, Katherine Ann Miller requests that she be known by her maiden name of Katherine Ann Van Dyk. She states that she has sufficient income to raise the child, Grace Elizabeth Miller, and does not request any monies to raise the child. No attempt shall be made for visitation from the father, Joseph William Miller. The child's name shall be Grace Elizabeth Van Dyk."

There was more, but it was legal writing that Karen didn't understand. The important thing was that she now had the address of the Van Dyk estate.

Karen sighed. What kind of woman refused to have her child know her father? Perhaps it wasn't Katie's idea, but a condition of her parents for Katie and Grace to live with them and be near the big city of Chicago, as Katie wanted. It sounded like Katie wouldn't have to worry about money.

Karen decided to go to Chicago, or rather to Oak Park, and do some investigating of her own. Since Ryan and his parents, Grandma Rose and Jack, were expecting her for Spring break, she needed to let them know right away that she wasn't going to Iowa on Spring Break. First she called Grandma Rose and explained what the letter said. Then she emailed Jack.

Dear Jack,
I need to meet Henrietta to find out more information about my sister. I know it's a long shot. Henrietta may not be employed by the Van Dyk's. The family may have moved. Who knows what has happened to Katie and Grace? I plan to talk to neighbors too. I told this to Grandma Rose. She said, "God knows. Go with God."
  Your friend,
  Karen

Jack's answer came an hour later.

Dear Karen,
I am sorry that we won't spend Spring Break together, but I have a great idea. Why don't I come to San Diego to spend time with you? I can come on Friday, the 8ᵗʰ of March, after my morning classes. Then on the 11ᵗʰ, you can fly to Chicago and I will fly back to Iowa.
  Will that work for you? Can you pick me up at the Lindbergh Field San Diego International Airport?
  PLEASE SAY, "YES." I can't wait to see you!!!
  Jack

Dear Jack,
YES! I haven't made my airplane reservation yet but flights are usually less expensive on Monday rather than Saturday.
  It will be good to see you and show you a little of my state.
  Karen

Chapter 22

Jack arrived at the airport in San Diego at four in the afternoon on Friday, the eighth of March. The timing was perfect for Karen because her classes let out at three thirty. She knew it would take time for Jack to get his luggage, so she should arrive at the airport to pick him up at about the same time he was ready to exit.

Jack had a big smile on his face as he stood at the drop off area outside the airport. Soon Karen pulled up in her Honda. He dropped his suitcase and held out both arms to give her a hug. She pushed the button to open her trunk and stepped out of the car to give him a brief hug. Someone honked their horn at them, so Jack threw the suitcase into the trunk and jumped into the car. Karen drove her Honda into the traffic that led to the Freeway on Interstate 5.

Karen explained, "We can sit in the car and watch the stalled rush hour traffic or we can stop at a little restaurant and wait for traffic to subside."

Jack was hungry so he gratefully said, "Please, let's go eat. Is traffic always this bad?"

"Only during rush hour." Karen said with laughter in her voice. This country boy had a lot to learn about city living.

Layers of cars and trucks were beneath them going in circles. "I usually get to the restaurant from the other direction. The restaurant is only a few blocks away, but I'm not sure how to get there from here. What exit should I use to get there?"

Jack realized that it was a rhetorical question, so he didn't answer. After taking the next exit, they learned that it was one way going in the wrong direction. Finally, they turned around and found the restaurant.

They were seated at a table by the window where Jack could see traffic whizzing overhead. "I have never seen traffic like this even in Des Moines."

Karen laughed. "You get used to it."

After they ordered a large pizza and sodas, Karen asked, "Is there any place special you want to go tomorrow?"

"You know the area. You choose." Jack answered.

"Okay, we will go to Point Loma, see the Pacific Ocean, the lighthouse, and then to the Silver Strand. If you were here longer, we could go to the Vallecito Mountains, but you leave on Monday to go back to Iowa and I will be on Spring Break heading to Chicago. Have you ever been to the mountains or ocean?"

"No, but I have been to see Lake Superior and Lake Michigan in the fall when the maple leaves turn crimson and bright orange and the oak leaves are orange while the birch and ash trees are a vivid yellow. Do the leaves turn colors here in San Diego?"

"No, we have mostly Palm trees, and even the Joshua trees in nearby Arizona are green. If someone plants a deciduous tree, the leaves turn brown and gradually fall off before spring."

"We live about four miles from Rathburn Lake and about thirty - five miles from Red Rock Lake. The Des Moines River is closer to us but the dam is by Pella, which makes the Red Rock Lake. We have many rivers in Iowa. Remember that Iowa is the land between two huge rivers - the Mississippi and the Missouri."

Soon they reached Park Blvd. and the tiny apartment where Karen and her nurse friend, Marsha, lived. Karen taught fourth grade, but Marsha worked different shifts so they weren't together very often. The apartment had a tiny kitchen area with a counter and three stools dividing it from the living room, which held a sofa and one chair. The bedroom had bunk beds and two chests of drawers with one large closet. A tiny bathroom was off the living room.

Karen pointed to the sofa and said, "You will need to sleep on the sofa. I think that it makes into a bed, but I've never tried to make that happen. Sorry that I don't have a larger apartment."

Jack responded, "That's okay. I'm just glad to see you."

They sat close together on the sofa and watched several movies that were recorded on the TV. Karen made popcorn as she explained, "I never watch movies without popcorn."

A little after midnight, Marsha came home from work. "So this is your very good friend from Iowa." She said, "He is a handsome man."

Karen blushed as she introduced Marsha to Jack.

Marsha continued, "It was a very tough night at the burn center. I was the charge nurse tonight so I didn't get much of a chance to eat. There was a wild fire up in Vallecito Mountains. . . . I'm going to eat some of the lasagna and go to bed."

Karen asked how many people were burned.

"Nine persons were taken by ambulance to our hospital. Two were taken to hydrotherapy to wash off their charred skin and then taken to their rooms. Five people were taken to hydrotherapy with 20 percent burns or more and then went to operating rooms. Two patients were mostly victims of smoke inhalation and given IV's and oxygen, but we needed to keep a sharp eye on them to see if they needed to be put on a ventilator."

Jack asked, "How does hydrotherapy work?"

Marsha answered. "Prior to hydrotherapy, the patients are given large doses of pain killers, while they are in their room. Then, we put the burn victims on a steel gurney and take them to the hydrotherapy room in the burn center. It has hoses with barely warm water and liquid soap. We gently wash the wounds and then apply creams and bandages. After they are taken to their rooms, the nurses wrap the patients in warm blankets, and tell them to rest.

"A funny story is told to the staff that there was a man who was inebriated and burned in a car accident before he was brought to the burn center by ambulance. The next day the man asked his family, 'Do you know what they did to me last night?'

"They answered, 'No.'"

The burned man said. "They put me on the hood of a police car and drove me through a car wash."

Karen said, "It sounds like you had an awful night."

When Marsha finished eating and retired to the bedroom, Karen helped Jack set up the sofa bed and brought him sheets and a blanket. They were both tired, so they retired too.

Chapter 23

The next morning, they were quiet as they left the apartment, so Marsha could sleep in. They decided to go to Mc Donald's for breakfast, so they wouldn't disturb Marsha.

They could smell smoke from last night's fire as soon as they stepped outdoors. Soon they were at Cabrillo Memorial Drive. To the east they could see the U.S. Naval Air Station. They parked by the Cabrillo National Monument. Karen took her binoculars and two water bottles from the Honda before they hiked to Point Loma.

Suddenly she squealed. "Look at that dot over to the west."

She handed her binoculars to Jack. Sure enough, there were two grey whales swimming in the ocean. The larger whale floated on the water. Seconds later, the smaller whale was floating. Then the large whale flipped into the ar. The small gray whale also flipped into the air. Next they saw the tails of both whales. Karen explained, "The grey whales come from Alaska in November to have their babies in the Baja area and swim back to Alaska in February. We just saw the mother whale teaching her baby how to follow her. These whales are later than most to migrate back to Alaska, but I'm so glad that we saw them. "You don't see whales in Iowa." added Karen.

"No, but I've never seen wild fires either." answered Jack.

They returned to the car, but didn't move it as they played the game of which was the best state.

Both Karen and Jack alternated responses.

"No, but you have tornadoes."

"You have earthquakes and tsunamis."

"We have whales and seals and porpoises."

"Iowa has deer, wild turkeys, raccoons, rabbits and squirrels."

"California has vineyards and citrus trees."

"The Midwest is the bread basket of the U.S.A. . . . We have four seasons."

"But it is warm here in the winter."

"I would rather have four seasons."

"What is this? A contest to see which state is best?"

"No."

Jack's face became serious as he answered, "I just want you to see the blessings of Iowa. Seriously, do you think you could live in Iowa? I see a future with us married and living together."

"Is this a proposal of marriage?" asked Karen.

Jack answered, "The problem is that I want to be a veterinary doctor. I have three more years of college."

Karen responded, "The timing isn't right. It's too soon. Let's be friends and give me time to find my father and sister."

Chapter 24

Marsha drove Karen and Jack to the San Diego Airport in the Honda that she owned jointly with Karen. That way, she had use of the car while Karen was away and they would not have to pay parking fees at the airport.

If the distance was short, they often rode their bicycles. Marsha had talked Karen into riding them. "It's healthier for you to walk or ride a bike," Marsha said. "Besides that, you don't have to deal with traffic; just go on the bike paths. "You don't have to deal with parking; you just lock it up to a light post."

Karen felt exhausted from rushing to the airport and saying good-bye to Jack. Once she was in the air, she felt butterflies as she flew to Chicago Midway Airport. It wasn't that she was afraid of flying or traffic. She was a city girl. She was afraid that this trip would be for nothing. Eighteen years is a long time to stay in the same house in the same neighborhood. What if they slammed the door in her face like they did to her father and Grandpa George?

When she landed, she grabbed her take - on bag and went to the entry of the airport to find a taxi to the motel. She was happy that she had made reservations. She laughed. It certainly wouldn't do to show up at the grand house with a carry-on bag over her shoulder. After check-in, she walked to the nearest restaurant for her favorite meal – fish and chips. She thought about walking a bit toward the park she saw in the distance but decided to return to her room before it got dark, since she didn't know the neighborhood.

After a long soak in the bathtub, she was so tired that she had no trouble falling asleep.

She was startled awake when her cell phone rang.

"Yes, I'm fine. I'm in my motel room snoozing. . . . Yes, I ate fish and chips and a salad in the nearby restaurant. You know that they don't serve much food on the plane. Sorry that I didn't let you know that I'm okay. . . . Please tell Grandma Rose, that I'm okay. . . . No, I didn't try to go to the Van Dyk house. That's for tomorrow. . . . Tell Grandma I'm glad that she is praying for me. Good night. Jack."

The next morning, she primped in front of the mirror. She put her light brown hair up in a messy pony tail. Her make-up was applied lightly. Again she wished that her nose was a little longer and her lips weren't so full. She chose a pink silk blouse, a flowered skirt, and her white sandals. She was ready.

The taxi ride wasn't long enough. She was at the double doors of the front of the house before she was ready.

The white haired woman who answered the door looked startled, almost like she had seen a ghost. "May I help you miss?"

"I'm Karen Miller Wells," she stammered.

"Pardon me, but you look like someone I know," the woman said.

Karen noticed the apron and asked, "Are you Henrietta Jones?"

"Why yes, how did you know?"

"You spoke with my grandmother, Rose Miller, once. I'm the daughter of Joe Miller from his first wife, Alice."

Henrietta gasped. "I want to talk to you but not here. Can we meet in a restaurant after I get off work?"

Henrietta gave her the directions to a little place that Mrs. Van Dyk would never go.

Karen asked, "Would you call me a cab? I need to go to my motel room."

"Of course, Miss. . . .You look like her, you know."

"Who?"

"Your sister, or should I say your half - sister."

Chapter 25

Karen walked to the little park near her motel room. The huge maple and oak trees shaded the bench where she sat. The plan was to meet Henrietta at the same restaurant where Karen ate last night, after Henrietta had prepared supper for the Van Dyk family. Time dragged on. She read some brochures from the motel, on local activities for tourists, but her mind couldn't concentrate on them.

She saw the white haired woman arrive by the bus stop a little way away. She was sure it was Henrietta.

The woman looked around until she spotted Karen and then came toward her in a fast trot. After seating herself beside Karen on the bench, Henrietta said, "I'm sure that you want to meet Grace. The trouble is, Grace doesn't know you exist. I think that Grace will want to meet you because she has often said that she wishes she wasn't an only child."

"Does Grace know our father?" Karen asked.

"No. Grace was told that her father was a farmer in Iowa who didn't want children. Grace was told that when Joe learned that his wife was pregnant, he ran away, so Katie came home to her parents.

Years later, Katie's father died in a car accident. Then Katie married an old man with congestive heart failure. He died two years later. Katie inherited large sums of money from both her husband and father.

"Now, it is only Katie's mother, Katie, and Grace who live here. Katie never learned how to cook or keep house, so I stayed on as a housekeeper for them."

Alice Boender Miller died soon after giving birth to Karen. "My brother and I were raised by my maternal aunt and uncle in California, but we were never adopted. My aunt and uncle never told us that they were not our parents, but gave us their last names of Wells.

That night, I heard another big fight between Joe and Ellen. Ellen refused to let us out of her sight. We couldn't even accompany Joe and Katie to the zoo. My brother, Jim, was angry too, because he wanted to go to the zoo."

"I met my father, once, when I was three - years - old. He and Katie came to California to see us. I remember it because my aunt, Ellen, cried for days before my dad and Katie visited us. Recently, my Grandma Rose, told me that Joe had planned to bring my brother and me to Iowa to live with him and Katie. After seeing us, Katie refused to allow us to live with her and Joe. She had no experience with children, and probably suspected that she was pregnant.

"It must have been shortly after Katie and Joe returned to Iowa, that Katie called her parents. They bought a train ticket for Katie to return to her parents' home."

Karen asked, "Was it Katie who refused to see Joe when he followed her to Chicago?"

"No. I answered the door. After the brief conversation, Mrs. Van Dyk came to the door and said that she didn't know any Joe Miller. Then, Mrs. Van Dyk slammed the door in his face! She told me that the man was probably Katie's husband. I was never to tell Katie that Joe had come to see her. Also, I was never to allow Joe to come into the house. I didn't think that was right but I needed to keep my job.

"Katie's parents arranged for the divorce after your grandfather, George, arrived to see Katie."

100

Henrietta changed the subject again. "You mentioned a brother. Does he know about Grace?"

"No. Jim was in the army and died in Afghanistan before I learned that Ellen and Matt were not my parents."

"I am sorry."

"Was it your grandmother, Rose, who told you about us?"

"She did, after I went to Iowa, but I never knew my grandmother before that. Grandma Rose and her daughter Ellen became estranged after Ellen refused to let us live with our father. It was a DNA test that said that I had similar DNA to my cousin, Ryan Miller. I contacted Ryan, who talked to Grandma Rose. I was invited to Iowa. I never felt so much at home as when I was there last summer. I spent Christmas with them in Iowa too."

Henrietta said, "Grace is a lonely person. I think she will be glad that she has more family, but has been taught never to trust strangers. I think it is best if I talk to Grace first and tell her about you and your father, grandparents and cousins."

"Will you do it soon? I am on Spring break from my job of teaching school. I really would like to meet Grace before I go back to California on Saturday."

Henrietta answered, "Grace needs to know about her other family. She is busy now with prom and graduation from high school this May, but I will talk to her tomorrow and ask her to meet you at this restaurant on Thursday. I need your phone number."

"Sure. That should be okay. It's 616 - 251 - 6546. I wrote it on this piece of paper. I will be waiting for your call."

The next morning, Karen took a quick shower because she didn't want to miss the phone call. She thought, *"I'm not sure when Henrietta can talk to Grace. When will I get the answer whether or not Grace wants to see me? What if Grace had other plans?"*

When Karen didn't get a call by noon, she decided to go to Lake Shore Drive and find the 49th Street Beach. Lying on the beach and watching the waves on Lake Michigan was something she could do and still get a phone call. At three thirty, a call came. Karen didn't recognize Henrietta's phone number, but answered anyway.

"Hello, this is Karen."

An excited voice asked, "Are you my sister, Karen?"

"Yes, if you are Grace Elizabeth Van Dyk."

"Where are you?" inquired Grace.

"I'm at the 49th Street Beach."

"May I come now?"

"Sure. I came from California to meet you." replied Karen.

"Mom is expecting me home for dinner, since she has a new friend that she wants me to meet. My friend, Sally, has a car, so she can drive me to the beach. . . . How will I know you?"

Karen answered, "I'm five foot five inches tall, with light brown hair in a messy pony tail and wearing jeans and a red shirt and a red hat."

"You have got to be kidding. I'm five foot seven inches tall with light brown hair in a messy pony tail, wearing a red shirt and jeans, but no hat. Do you have blue eyes?"

"Yes."

"We will be there soon."

Twenty minutes later a green Suzuki drove into the parking lot. Two girls popped out and ran to Karen, who was waiting for them at the edge of the parking lot.

Sally stared at them and said, "You two look like sisters!"

Simultaneously, both answered. "We are sisters."

Karen told Grace what she knew about their father. They joyously answered each other's questions. It was funny, the way Sally bobbed her head looking at one and then the other.

Grace said that Friday, the next night, was prom night. She was the head of the committee to decorate the gym and then she was going to prom and to the overnight party. It would be impossible for her to see Karen before Karen had to go to the airport.

Sally reminded Grace that they better go to Grace's house, if she was going to dress for dinner.

Grace told Karen, "Mom wouldn't introduce this guy to me if she wasn't serious about him. I really have to go, but may I hug you first?"

Karen held out her arms for a hug.

Karen said, "Don't lose my phone number."

Grace answered. "I won't, but if I do, Henrietta will give it to me. She will be so happy that we met. . . . You have my number from when I called you. Please put it in your contacts."

"Okay."

Karen watched Grace and Sally until they drove away. Then she walked to the bus stop to return to her motel room.

The first thing she did, after entering the room, was to phone Jack to tell him her good news. Then she called Grandma Rose and then Ryan.

Chapter 26

Karen's trip from the Chicago O Hare International Airport to the San Diego International Airport on Lindberg Field was uneventful.

Marsha was at the California airport to pick up Karen. They chatted about the reunion of Karen with her young sister, Grace.

Karen sent a message via the internet to Grace.

Dear Grace,

It was wonderful to meet you. I hope to see you this summer in Iowa, where you can meet your relatives, and we can spend time together. Is this possible?

Your new - found sister,

Karen Wells

The answer came the next day.

Dear Karen,

I talked to Henrietta. She had more information about our father and you. I feel like I want to know more about you and my heritage.

Yes, I'm looking forward to going to Iowa!!

A lot of things have changed since we saw each other.

I received a new Toyota Camry SE Hybrid car, as a graduation present. The color is called celestial silver metallic with a midnight black metallic roof. It has all the bells and whistles. The car is a 2.5 L —

4 cylinder with an 8 speed automatic transmission. It can get 28 to 39 mpg. It even has a cold weather package for the Chicago area, which includes heated seats, a heated steering wheel, and even heated side view windows. Of course, I won't need heat in Iowa in the summer.

Now I have the freedom to go where I want to go. I'm almost 18, so I will soon be an adult.

Another change is that Mother is happier than I have ever known her to be. I think she is in love. Anyway, Bill, the man my mom wanted me to meet, wants to take her on a European cruise this summer. Mother asked if I wanted to come along too. Can you imagine me chaperoning her? Instead, I asked if I could go to Iowa with my friend, Sally. It was a white lie.

I said that Sally had relatives there that she wanted to visit, but you know that it is me that wants to go to Iowa to meet my cousins and learn more about my dad.

Sally's parents are fine with the trip, as long as we are together, and it isn't too expensive. Sally was jumping up and down when I told her about the trip.

Now I need the name and address of a fancy place where we can stay. Mother would never let me go if she thought that I didn't have decent accommodations. She would never let me stay on a farm. Also, I don't think there would be room at the farm for both Sally and me. When I last talked to you on the phone, you said that you will be on the farm. Besides, I want Mom and Grandma Van Dyk to pay for it.

Please send me some information on a nice place to stay.

Your sister,
Grace

Dear Grace,

The best place around here, where you would want to stay, is Honey Creek Resort. It is located on Rathbun Lake and only a few miles from the farm. It's about 20 miles from Albia and about 20 miles from Centerville. Ottumwa is about 45 miles away. These towns are county seats and are the largest towns around us. The farm is located in Monroe County, which has such a low population that it doesn't even have a Walmart.

We are fortunate that Rathbun Lake area has Honey Creek Resort. While at the resort, you could swim, golf, and use Wi-Fi. Since you are staying there, breakfast is included, and their restaurant is first class for other meals. I know because I have eaten there several times with Jack and Ryan.

This non-smoking hotel, even has laundry service. The best thing you can do is look up Honey Creek Resorts *on the web and show the wonderful photos to your mother.*

It would be ideal if you stay there. You and Sally could do things together and you could go places with my family. Oops. I mean our family. I want to get to know you better too.

Your sister,
Karen

Grace answered Karen the next day.

Dear Karen,
I showed Mom the web site of Honey Creek Resorts. She loved it. She made reservations for June 3 to the 30ᵗʰ for Sally and me. That is when Mom is leaving for her European vacation. I really don't think she wanted me along on the cruise.
Thank you for finding this resort.
It sounds like it is a very nice place. Sally is excited too. We plan to drive there in one day. We will leave in the morning and arrive by 4pm., which is the check - in time. We will explore Honey Creek Resort and the restaurant. Hope to see you on the 4th of June, if that is okay with you.
Your sister,
Grace

Karen sat down by her computer and answered her sister immediately.

Dear Grace,

Wonderful! I will be at Grandma Rose's home on the 3rd, but I need to be picked up from the airport in Des Moines, so I don't know what time I will arrive at the farm.

After I talk with Grandma, I will find out when we can meet with Aunt Mary and find out what we can about her brother and our father.

See you soon.

Your sister,

Karen

June 3rd was a beautiful day for Karen to fly from San Diego, and for Grace to drive from the Chicago area. Grace called Karen to tell her that Sally and she had arrived safely to Honey Creek Resorts.

Karen answered that she was on her way to the farm from Des Moines. Everyone was tired.

The next morning, when the Grace and Sally arrived at the farm, everyone was so surprised that Karen and Grace looked so much alike.

It was hard to tell who was the happiest to see Karen: Jack, Grace, or Grandma Rose. They all had such smiles on their faces.

Ryan drove Grandma Rose to the farm where Mary Miller lived to ask when Karen and Grace could meet her. She answered, "Why not now?"

First, Ryan phoned the girls to be ready for the meeting. Then, Mary, Grandma Rose, and Ryan got into the car and the three of them returned to the Boender farm.

Grace asked, "Is it okay for us to be wearing jeans when we meet her?"

Karen answered, "Don't worry. Aunt Mary will be wearing Amish clothing, but she knows that young girls wear 'English clothes'. Grandma Rose says that our aunt is very comfortable to be with and wants to know about us. She won't be worrying about our clothing."

Chapter 27

There was such a contrast among the women sitting around Grandma Rose's table. The two older women, Grandma Rose and Mary Miller, wore long dresses to their ankles covered with aprons. They wore socks and black heavy shoes. Grandma's hair was in a bun on top of her head, while you couldn't see Mary's hair because she wore an Amish cap.

Both blue eyed sisters, Grace and Karen, wore jeans and t – shirts, and sandals on their feet. They had long blond hair tied along the back of their necks.

Karen asked Mary, "What was our father like as a younger brother?"

Mary answered, "He liked to have fun and didn't do his chores if he could get someone else to do them for him. Sometimes he would barter with his brothers or me, with his dessert, or just beg us to do his work. He didn't like farm work, but often went to see John Mast work on his furniture. Old man Mast would give him pieces of wood to whittle on. Joe was 'happy and go lucky', as you English would say.

"Joe loved to tease his sisters. I remember him chasing Faith with a garden snake. She was terrified. . . . I wonder if he is happy now!"

Karen said, "I wouldn't like anything to do with snakes either. . . . When is the last time anyone heard from Joe?"

Mary answered. "Eli, our brother, got a note from Joe after he visited your mother's house. It said to tell Mother that he was well but not coming home. When our Mother died, Eli came home for the funeral, but Joe didn't come. Eli said, that Joe had told him, that Joe's presence at the funeral might cause a disturbance. He didn't want to do that to Mother."

Karen asked, "Would Eli know where our father is?"

"Mary answered, "I don't know."

Grace asked, "I wonder, does he even know that I was born?"

Again Mary answered, "I don't know. Of course, I knew about Karen because I knew that her mother died, but I didn't know about you, Grace. . . . I can see that you both have Joe's blue eyes."

Karen answered, "Thank you. Do you know where Eli is now?"

Mary said, "He went to Indiana and married a nice Amish girl and worked at a factory making recreational vehicles. I think that recreational vehicles are moving things that look like trucks or buses. People travel and live in them."

Karen excitedly asked, "Do you know where the factory is?"

Mary answered, "The name of the factory was Jay something. I remember because my middle name is Jane, so I remember J or J-A-Y."

Karen answered, "Thank you for the information. If you remember anything else to help us find him, please let Grandma know. She will tell us."

Mary answered, "I will."

Grandma Rose said, "It will be awhile before Ryan can take you home. Please stay for a cup of tea and some of the cinnamon rolls that I made this morning."

"Could we go in the living room? I can eat at that little side table. I'm not supposed to eat with you since you are no longer Amish."

Grace said, "Who would know?"

Mary answered, "I would know. I try not to do anything the bishop would disapprove of."

Grace asked, "Would he disapprove if you invited us to go to your house and meet some cousins?"

"I will ask him."

Ryan knocked on the door, opened it, as he called. "Is anyone home?"

"Come in." Grandma said. Sally and Jake entered the house with Ryan.

"Sally, where have you been?" questioned Grace.

Ryan answered, "She went riding with Jack. Sally rode on Prince, while Jack rode on his new horse."

That's funny, thought Karen. He didn't tell me that he had a new horse. She felt a tinge of jealousy, but she was antsy to go to her computer and look up RV manufactures in Indiana. Now she needed to wait until Mary went home.

Mary turned to Karen and said, "If you find Joe, tell him that I love him and want to see him."

Karen said, "Yes. I will."

"Are you ready to return home?" Ryan asked Mary.

She said, "Yes."

"Karen, Sally and Grace, do you three want to ride along?" Ryan said.

"I want to work on my computer," Karen answered.

After the others left, Grandma said, "I think that I'll lie down for a while, as she turned to go to the bedroom."

Karen put her computer on the kitchen table and looked up the names of Indiana RV manufacturers.

Karen learned that the manufacturer of RV's in Indiana, who's name started with 'Jay,' was most likely JayCo. The factory was located in Middlebury, Indiana. It was started by Lloyd Jay Bontrager in 1968, after he received the patent for his pop - up camper. At one time, 70% of the factory workers were Amish or Mennonite.

Karen liked that they were a green manufacturer with a governor's award of excellence. She also liked the idea of the blue jay as their mascot and logo. Could this be where Eli Miller worked?

When the young people returned, Karen asked, "Does anyone want to go to Indiana with me to do a tour of the Jayco factory?

"They are closed the week of June 30 to July 6, so I think that we should go before June 30. I'd like to go June 23."

Sally looked at Ryan and said. "I think that we should stay here, since we have reservations at the Honey Creek Resort through the 30th.

Grace answered, "You are probably right. Mom will be upset when she gets the bill if she finds out that we haven't stayed at the Honey Creek Resort the whole time. . . . I'm not too thrilled to go on a factory tour."

"We should probably drive since it's not too far. The factory is off Highway 107 on Interstate 80-90 Illinois and Indiana toll way."

"I want to go with you," Jack said.

Ryan said. "You can take the old Chevy truck if you want to since Karen never learned to drive a straight stick car."

Ryan added, "I want to take these two young ladies to see Pella and the Amish by Cantril. I want to ride in Grace's Toyota."

"Are you game for that?" Jack asked all the young people.

"That would be okay with me," answered Karen. She added, "I need to buy some new shoes. They don't allow you to take the tour wearing flip flops, sandals, or opened toed shoes. That's all I have with me."

Chapter 28

The old truck was a comfort to Jack. He liked driving it, the farther the better. The stick shift and clutch made him feel powerful. He looked over to Karen and thought that it was a nice day to travel with a beautiful girl beside him.

Karen watched him shift gears and said, "I'm glad that you are driving. I never learned to drive a stick."

"That's why you need me." Jack smiled. He added, "Isn't it funny that George put the cover over the truck bed and added sleeping bags?"

"I don't think we will need sleeping bags, since I have the money to stay in motels." Karen answered. "It is good that Grandma Rose gave us all this food to picnic with. We can stop at a rest area whenever you are hungry."

She observed the blue sky with white clouds and the fields that were green with new crops of oats, corn and soybeans. "San Diego has a lot of parks and places to go to the beach, but the beauty of June in Iowa is great too."

Simultaneously, they quoted Grandma Rose, "Isn't this a beautiful day that God has made."

It was good to laugh.

Jack checked the gas gauge and odometer before he answered. "I guess you get used to it. I don't think about it very much."

They rambled on down the road in silence as they crossed Illinois. Then Karen asked, "Do you get tornadoes and cloud bursts much in the summer?"

Jack answered, "Ah, Karen, it hasn't rained for six weeks. Let's not worry about a storm."

He no sooner said that when a few drops of rain hit the windshield.

They stopped chatting because the rain became more intense and was making it hard to see the highway. Jack slowed down. The highway was slick from the oil that had risen to the top of the blacktop. The rain turned to hail. It sounded like a hammer was hitting the windshield and sides of the truck.

Jack spied a gravel road with trees off the wide shoulders. The hail was the size of golf balls.

Jack explained, "I don't hear thunder, so I don't suppose lightning will hit the trees. It should be safe to park there. The trees may save the windshield."

Fifteen minutes later, the hail stopped. They looked at the shredded leaves and debris that had blown around them. It included a few shingles off the roof of a house that was in front of them. They didn't know it, but what Jack thought was a road was actually a driveway.

They sat for a few minutes wondering if the storm was over. Jack got out of the truck and looked for damage. The truck had a few more dents, but was okay.

"Look over there." Karen pointed to a man dressed in the home-made shirt and pants with suspenders and wearing high boots.

The man looked at his roof and then all around him. He spied the strangers in the truck. Running toward them, he shouted, "STOP! The bridge may be out below the hill. It has happened before when we had a huge amount of rain. You need to come inside our house and rest a bit. I'll take the horse down the hill to check the bridge."

Reaching the porch, someone opened the door and yelled, "Come in quick and take off your muddy shoes." The speaker was a blued eyed blonde girl of about eight years old. "Boots are needed here," she added. The mother gave the child a dirty look.

The aproned woman, of about thirty years, added, "Please sit by our table and have a cup of hot tea."

"Thank you kindly." Jack answered.

The mother of the child asked, "Where are you going?" as she prepared the tea in a white teapot.

"We have reservations at the JayCo factory tomorrow," Jack answered.

"Where are you from?" she continued.

"I live near Moravia, Iowa, near a little village of Forest Grove," he answered.

"We know some people near there on a farm." The woman answered. "They are the Yoders and the Millers and –

Karen gasped, "We are looking for Eli and James Miller," she said.

The woman replied, "I knew the Millers. One was named Mary Miller, but I don't know if they are still living in Iowa."

"My grandmother, Rose, was a Miller before she married a Boender."

"Yah, she married a Dutchman," the woman responded. "My grandmother and Rose were best friends before Rose married."

"I was raised by my aunt and uncle, but we are looking for my father who is Joseph or Joe Miller," Karen explained. "Mary Miller thought that he works for Jayco."

The door opened and a soaking wet man entered and slammed the door, as he kicked off his boots. He handed his shirt to his wife, who hung it on a chair near the fireplace.

When he sat in the chair by the table, his wife handed him a cup of tea without his asking for it. Everyone waited for him to speak. "The bridge is good. Where are you going?"

Jack told him about the trip to the JayCo factory. "We are looking for Eli and James Miller, who are related to Karen."

"I don't know how to get there, but I think it is north and east of here," the man explained.

"Yes," Karen said. "The GPS said to go to the road on Interstate 80/ 90 on Illinois/ Indiana, which is a toll road. Then we need to take the exit for 107."

The man shook his head. "What's a GPS?"

Jack explained that it is a system in the car that acts as a map to tell you where you are going.

"You need to turn around and when you come to the next road, turn left and travel north."

"Thank you for your help," Karen said as she and Jack stood up to go.

"God be with you. I hope you find your family. Say hello to the Millers and your grandma, Rose, from the Borntragers," the woman said.

Chapter 29

Karen phoned Jack from her motel room to see what time he wanted to go for the hot breakfast in the dining area near the check-out area.

The coffee was good, as well as the waffles with jam or syrup. Orange and apple juice were available, but no other fruit. Karen opened the packet of oatmeal, added water and put it in the microwave. It didn't taste as good as her grandmother's oatmeal. Grandma Rose added cranberries and pecans to her oatmeal.

They were early for their appointment to tour the factory so they rode around Middlebury, but the town was very small. Ryan filled the gas tank and a can he found in the back of the pickup with gasoline.

They were sitting in the little waiting room, before the tour, when eight other people started asking each other where they had been and where they were going. Apparently, RVers, as they called themselves, were very friendly toward strangers.

Jack said they were from Iowa and California and added that they weren't in the market for a new RV, but were trying to find Eli and Joseph Miller. "We heard that they worked here, but we had no idea the plant was so big."

Karen added, "They are relatives of mine."

The receptionist overheard them. "I know an Eli Miller. He is a supervisor here, but there are so many Millers. He might not be the one you are looking for."

Karen jumped up and ran to the receptionist desk and whispered, "Could you please contact him and ask if we could see him? PLEASE!"

Before the receptionist answered, a man came into the room and handed each person a helmet. He said, "This way, please."

All the observers entered the huge room filled with metal rectangles on wheels. "We will see the RVs built on a van chassis."

When he saw the perplexed look on some of the women's faces, he added. "A chassis is the foundation that supports the body and engine of a vehicle. Some RV's are built on semi or bus chassis."

Karen saw that the wheels were already attached. Now people were welding metal, or plastic. boxes in place on the chassis and placing the engine components in place.

The boxes were explained to be holding tanks for fresh, grey, and black water. Other supports were welded into this foundation.

Further down the line, the subfloor was put into place. Then a huge piece of vinyl was added. Some furniture and appliances, and all the cupboards and cabinets, were added before the walls. The walls were covered with vinyl wallpaper before they were set into place. Now there were floor coverings under all the cabinets and on the floors. The flooring was without seams because the vinyl was so big. Wallpaper was also on the walls behind the cabinets.

It seemed amazing to Jack that all the furniture in a house, and all the common appliances could be made smaller to fit into such small spaces. Karen saw that too, but her mind teeter tottered between the tour and wondering if they would find Eli and her father.

"Please God," She prayed. "Help me find them."

She felt more calm and again noticed what the tour guide was explaining. The storage areas were amazing. Of course you could not put a month's worth of groceries in the RV, but a week or two would fit nicely.

The biggest surprise was how everything was put in place before the ceiling and roof were added.

Further down the line was a completed RV being driven out of the building. The tour was over.

The tour guide led them to the front of the building. "Thank you for taking the tour. If you want more information, return to the reception area for brochures. I will be there to answer questions."

Jack looked at Karen. "Do you want to go in?" He asked.

"Yes." Karen answered. "Let's find out what the receptionist knows about Eli and Joe."

Chapter 30

Karen ran inside the waiting room to the receptionist's desk. "Did you call Eli Miller?"

The receptionist just nodded her head toward the man who stood in the corner.

Karen just stared at the man who wore jeans and a button down dress shirt. It was hard to see his hair, since he wore a helmet, but he looked so much like pictures that she had seen of her father.

The man walked up to her and said, "I'm Eli Miller. . . . I understand you want to see me."

"I'm mm." Karen stammered. "I'm Karen Wells, but I was born a Miller."

"Is this your husband?"

"No. Jack is a friend and a neighbor to my grandmother, Rose Boender. Your sister, Mary Miller, is a friend of Grandma's. I'm looking for my father, Joseph Miller."

"How are they – my sister and your grandmother?"

"They are fine, but Grandma Rose has some trouble walking and her endurance is low. My great aunt Mary was fine when we had tea at Grandma's home a couple of weeks ago."

"But Mary is Amish and uses the old ways. I'm surprised that she would eat with Rose."

"Well, she sat at another table, but we talked a long time to each other."

"Why don't you sit down while I make some phone calls. Don't go away."

Karen turned and sat down beside Jack. *What is going to happen now?* She wondered.

Jack didn't say anything. Since he had heard the conversation with Eli, he too wondered what would happen next. He reached over and held Karen's cold hand. With his left hand he flipped the pages of the Jay Co brochure.

After a few minutes, which seemed like a long time to Karen, Eli returned.

"I made a phone call to my wife and asked her if you could meet us for supper at our home. She said 'yes'. She will call my brother, Joe, after work and invite him too."

Karen's face beamed. She wiped away a tear from her cheek as she turned to Jack.

"We can stay another day, can't we? I so want to meet my family."

Jack answered, "Absolutely."

Eli turned to Jack and gave him the address to where he lived.

"I need to get back to work now but I will see you at six o clock." Eli said.

Jack and Karen returned to the motel and asked for another night's accommodations.

The clerk said, "We are quite full, since it is so close to the 4th of July but we just had a cancellation. The two of you will have to stay in the same room. We could put twin beds in it if you want us to do that."

Jack turned to Karen. She just nodded her head.

"That will be fine." Jack said, "We would appreciate twin beds."

"Go in the next room, where you had breakfast, and have a cup of coffee. It will only take a few minutes."

They went into the dining room. Jack got his coffee but Karen said, "I'm too nervous to have caffeine now. I would like to take a hot tub bath when we get to our room."

Soon, someone came and told them that their room was ready. Jack took his coffee with him. When they got to their room, Karen used the bathroom to relax in the tub.

Soon, Jack knocked at the bathroom door and announced, "We had better get ready for tonight."

Karen opened her suitcase, which was in the bathroom, and changed into an ankle length sundress before letting Jack use the bathroom to change his shirt.

They arrived to a modest ranch type house. Eli answered the door and ushered them into the foyer. A pretty woman came to the door wearing an apron over her pink dress.

"Welcome." She said. "I'm Nellie. Pardon me while I finish in the kitchen."

Karen asked, "May I help you?"

"You may help set the table." As Nellie led the way to the kitchen, she stopped and called up the stairway. "Alice, come on down. Supper is almost ready."

"In a minute." The voice answered. Soon a barefoot girl, about 10 - years - old, wearing a long blue dress, raced down the stairs. She stopped when she saw Karen.

"Who are you?" The young girl asked.

Nellie answered for Karen. "We think that she is Uncle Joe's daughter."

"Alice was my mother's name," said Karen.

"We know." Alice handed the container of silverware to Karen. She asked, "Why didn't you come here before so we could be a family?"

Karen answered, "I didn't know where you lived."

"Alice, sit down." her mother told her."

Just then, four men entered the kitchen. After they bowed their heads and said a silent blessing, the mashed potatoes, roast beef, and green beans were passed around.

The stranger stared and stared at Karen after he sat down across from her. "Tell me about my kin," He finally said.

"I found out that my cousin, Ryan Boender, who lives in Iowa, was a close match to my DNA."

"What's DNA?" Inquired Alice. "It's something in your body and blood that tells who you are related to." answered Karen.

Karen added, "I contacted Ryan and asked if I could visit the family in Iowa. His dad is George Boender and his grandmother is Rose Boender. They agreed. Grandmother Rose told me that the woman, who I thought of as a mother, was really Rose's daughter and my Aunt Ellen. Alice Miller, my mother, was born to Grandma's other daughter. Alice, my mother, died shortly after my birth. My father, Joe Miller, couldn't take care of an infant and a three - year - old boy, and also provide for his children. When Ellen returned to California, she took my brother and me to live with her."

Joe questioned Karen. "Does your brother know about the grandparents?"

"No," answered Karen. "I only found out about my Miller family last year. My brother, Jim, died in Afghanistan several years ago, while he was in the army.

"Grandma Rose said that my father married again. My dad came to California, planning to return to Iowa, with his children. His new wife, Katie, decided that she didn't want his children to live with her and Joe. I don't know if Katie realized that she was pregnant or not, but when she returned to Iowa, she decided to visit her parents in Illinois. She never came back, but filed for divorce instead.

Joe went to Illinois, but returned to Iowa and then disappeared.

Joe spoke in a hoarse voice. "Do you know where Katie's child is now?"

Karen answered, "My sister is in Iowa visiting with Grandma Rose, her aunt Betty, uncle George, and our cousins." . . .

Eli said, "Congratulations! You really did a lot of research young lady."

Karen answered, "It is important to me to know my family."

Jack looked at Karen. She really looked exhausted! It had been an emotion packed evening!

Jack stood up and said, "Thank you for the delicious meal. I really think that we need to get to the motel and call it a night. We plan to leave before 7 in the morning."

Karen stood up and approached Joe. "May I hug you?" She asked. She put her arms around the stiff man, but he finally raised his right arm and patted her on her back.

She heard the whisper from Eli, "She has a lot of true facts and seems like the real thing."

The next morning Karen's phone rang shortly after 6:30 am. "Hello. Is this Karen? . . . This is Eli Miller. My brother and I talked most of the night. Apparently, the old lady, I mean Grandma Rose is sharp as she can be and bears him no ill will. Joe wants to see her and meet his other daughter. He has other kin near Moravia, too. Is it possible for him to ride with you to Iowa?"

Chapter 31

Jack took the phone from Karen and answered. "Of course, Joe can ride with us to Iowa, but we have an old truck without air conditioning. It only has a bench seat, so Joe will have to sit up front with us. It might be a little crowded."

Eli answered, "Joe really wants to see his daughters and spend time with them. He said he would even ride in the back."

Jack carried his and Karen's suitcases to the truck before returning to the motel for breakfast. After eating a big breakfast, they checked out. The man at the desk said, "You may fill your thermos with what is left of the coffee. I need to make a new pot anyway."

Jack and Karen drove in silence to Eli's house. Jack was surprised by the size of the two big boxes of Joe's belongings, but there was plenty of room in the back of the truck. Eli told Karen and Jack that he and Joe had spent the night talking and packing Joe's belongs. They were sure that the young people wouldn't go to all the trouble of finding Joe without agreeing to take Joe to Iowa.

Nellie gave them another box filled with food and a thermos filled with ice tea. She had added to the food that Joe had removed from his apartment, which was now in the truck.

Karen thought that apparently Joe planned to stay a long time in Iowa because he told Eli that he wanted someone to help load the rest of his stuff and put it in Eli's basement. She didn't mention it. Storing things in a basement was new to Karen, since they didn't have basements in San Diego.

Jack opened the door for Karen to sit in the middle and then he jumped into the driver's seat. Joe sat beside her next to the door.

Jack used the crank to open the window of the truck. Although the temperature had been cooled by the hail a couple of days ago, it was only about 85 degrees now. Joe watched Jack and then cranked the window down on the passenger's side of the truck.

Joe asked a few questions, but was otherwise silent. Soon he nodded off and was sound asleep.

Jack stopped at a gas station after they crossed the Mississippi River. Joe woke up and went with them into the gas station to use the bathroom. While Jack filled the fuel tank with diesel fuel, Karen purchased three Pepsi drinks. Joe asked if he could sleep in the back of the truck, since he had no sleep the night before. Jack unrolled the two sleeping bags and placed them beside the boxes. Now Joe had a make - shift mattress, so he could stretch out and would be more comfortable.

They had just passed an exit when suddenly there was a loud noise as cars and semis crashed in a multi - vehicle accident in front of them. Screams and the sounds of vehicle after vehicle crashing into each other were horrifying! Jack drove into a ditch.

Karen and Jack were both shaking when Joe knocked on the window and asked, "What happened?"

Jack just shook his head. "Help me push this truck to the shoulder!" He shouted. Joe helped push the truck around and jumped into the front seat. They headed back to the exit.

Jack drove down a two lane country road. After a mile or so down the road, he stopped so they could check things. Karen had a bruise on her right arm where she had been thrown against the door of the pickup. Joe had a bruise on his leg from his wild ride in the back of the truck, but was otherwise okay. Jack said that he wasn't hurt. The truck had another dent where they hit the ditch but it was still running. The stuff in the back of the pickup was jumbled together, but they didn't see anything leaking.

Karen said, "Thank God, we were not badly hurt!"

The GPS and their cell phones stopped working.

Since they didn't know where they were going, they decided to travel on the small roads and head south and west. They saw people standing in their yards with a dazed expression on their faces. Some were sobbing and holding on to their children. It was chaos!

At times, they saw a fire that people were trying to put out. Firetrucks were nowhere to be seen. People were surprised to see the pickup going down the road. There were more vehicles stopped on the road. Sometimes Jack and Joe had to stop and push a car far enough off the road so they could get by. People were walking along the road, but no one tried to stop them. The trio just kept slowly moving.

They wondered when they would get home, but were grateful that they had phoned Ryan and Grandma Rose last night to explain that they had found Joe, and would be getting home later than they had previously told Rose.

Chapter 32

Meanwhile, back at the farm, Betty removed the cake from the oven, when she saw a flash. The lights went out. She tried to heat a cup of coffee in the microwave, but that didn't work. She went to her cell phone to call George at the restaurant in Albia. He should be eating lunch now, since the golf game would be over. The cell phone wasn't working either.

Betty didn't know what to do!

She was alone in the house!

She remembered something about Ryan taking the girls site seeing in Pella.

Maybe she should see if the old lady was okay.

Rose wasn't in her house!

She spied Rose gathering lettuce, green onions, and radishes for a salad.

"Everyone is gone and none of the electricity works!" She cried and shouted.

Rose didn't know anything about the electricity being off!

Rose put her arm around the sobbing Betty and led her to the little house. "Sit down and we will have a cup of tea and talk about what is happening," Rose instructed.

"But the stove doesn't work," Betty exclaimed!

"My stove does." Grandma said. It was true that she had to light the igniter switch with one of her long matches, but the flame started.

Grandma took some potatoes from her cupboard, sat down across from Betty, and started to peel them. "Now tell me where everyone is." She instructed. Rose thought that if Betty knew where everyone was, and recited it; Betty would calm down.

Betty said. "Ryan took Ann, Grace, and Sally to Pella for an Independence Day celebration. They also talked about going to Bussey for the 4th of July parade. George is golfing with his friends. Jack took Karen to Indiana, to search for more of Karen's relatives.

Betty saw that Grandma Rose was now chopping up all the vegetables, except the lettuce. "What are you doing?" Betty asked. "You even cut up the radishes!"

"You won't know that they are radishes," Grandma explained. "I'm sure the others will be home before too long and they will be hungry. Soup lasts a long time, if I keep the heat setting on low. I was going to make a salad, but I can't let any vegetable go to waste if we have to survive a long time without electricity."

"You mean this could go on and on?" Betty pulled a face that was not very pleasant.

Rose stood up and walked to the refrigerator and got the left over chicken to add to the soup.

After she sat down to cut up the chicken, there was a knock on Grandma Rose's door. Betty whispered, "Do we want to open it?"

Rose didn't answer Betty, but gave her a dirty look before she rose to answer it.

It was the neighbor from a half mile away, who was Jack's father. He leaned the bicycle against the outside wall and anxiously asked, "Have you heard from Jack and Karen?"

"Not since they called last night." Grandma answered. "They said on the phone that they had found Karen's dad and were going to drive home in the morning."

"But the cars aren't running!" He sputtered.

"The old cars and trucks are working." Grandma explained. "They didn't have electronics go out, since the old truck was made before there were electronics used in cars and pickups." I'm more worried about Ryan and the girls. They took Grace's new car."

They sat in the living room and watched the road in front of Grandma's house. Traffic wasn't moving.

Then they heard the clip clop of horses. The horses stopped at the end of the driveway. Sitting on some tires, in a hay wagon, was George. He unloaded the tires and ran to his house. Since no one answered, Grandma ran to her door and yelled for George. "We are here."

George explained that Mark's car had stalled on Highway 14. He had walked to his Amish friend's house and got a ride home on his hay wagon pulled by his two horses. Mark then begged his friend to go to Highway 5 and pick up his friend George. George didn't have much cash on him, but promised to trade milk for the ride. Others, who were traveling north, also got a ride.

An hour later, the same horses and wagon came into the driveway. Jumping off of it were the girls and Ryan.

The Amish man introduced himself as Amos Yoder. He asked if he could water his horses. George went out to help him.

Jack explained that after he and the girls went to Pella, they went to Bussey. The parade was over but the Ferris wheel and kiddy rides were in the park. Grace wanted to ride on the Ferris wheel, so they all got onto the same seat and faced each other. The Ferris wheel started to go around. Suddenly, everything stopped. People were screaming! Things were flying everywhere!

They were not very high in the Ferris wheel, so they jumped off. They agreed to go to Grace's car. It was parked on the road near the park.

Someone had rear - ended it! The car wouldn't start! They got out and started walking toward home. A man driving horses and a wagon stopped and asked them if they were related to George Boender. They all said "Yes!"

"I just took Mr. Boender home," he stated. "Hop in and I will take you home."

Amos drove the horses around the block and headed west and then south. He stopped and picked up several people who were also walking south on Highway 5, but dropped them off before he got to the Boender's farm.

Grandma invited everyone to sit down and have soup, coffee and milk. Betty told Grace to go to the Boender house and get the cake that Betty had made as a celebration for the 4th of July.

Grandma Rose prayed out loud, as she thanked God for their safety and for Amos. They asked for blessing on the food and then helped themselves to a bowl of soup. There wasn't much room at the table, so Ryan sat between Grace and Sally on the sofa.

Chapter 33

J ack drove his truck heading west and then south. Sometimes, Jack, Karen, and her father, Joseph, ran into dead - end roads. Jack drove off the main roads, because there were so many vehicles stalled on the roads that he couldn't drive around them, without going into ditches.

They stopped at a little picnic area and the three of them ate food and drank ice tea that Eli's wife had given them. No one else was parked in the area, so Jack and Karen decided to stretch their legs and walk around the area.

After they were out of sight of Karen's father, Jack said, "I'm so glad that you are safe and we are together." He stopped. "I want to kiss you. Alright?"

Karen stepped closer to Jack and put her hands on Jack's shoulder and lifted her head in answer.

They kissed and stood close together for a minute. Jack murmured, "I don't know what I would do without you."

"I love you too." Karen answered.

"It's getting late. It will be dark soon. It will be dangerous to drive with so much debris on the road, and I'm so tired." Jack admitted.

Karen said, "Why don't we stay here for the night?"

"Okay," Jack said. "You sleep in the truck bed on the foam; your dad and I will sleep in sleeping bags beside the truck. . . . I think we will be safe here, but I'm afraid of looters."

When Jack, Karen, and Joseph woke the next morning, they saw an old camper parked at the end of the picnic area. No one appeared to be moving in it, so they stayed away from that camper.

The porta potty was welcome. Since there was no sink to wash up, Karen used a t-shirt as a face cloth and wet it with their water to wipe her face. Then she handed the shirt to Jack; he used it and then gave it to Karen's father.

Jack had shaved the day before, but Joe had a three-day growth beard. They couldn't shave very well in the road side park.

They ate crackers and peanut butter for breakfast. At 7:30 a.m., they resumed their trip. Again, Karen sat in the middle.

They turned around before they reached the Mississippi River. Now they were going west.

There was little conversation, but every now and then Joe would ask a question. Apparently, Joe was concerned about his reception. "I never told your grandma or aunt or uncle good-bye." Joe said. "I didn't want to tell them where I was going."

Karen tried to reassure him. "Grandma never holds a grudge and I never heard Uncle George or Aunt Betty say anything bad about you."

"I know where we are!" exclaimed Jack. "We are north of the Amana colonies. We must have gone in a circle somewhere. We are a little bit north of Interstate 80."

They drove south to exit number 220. Fortunately, the little used exit was clear of debris.

"How do we get to your farm?" asked Karen.

"We zig zag west toward Ottumwa on 149 and then west on Highway 34, then to Highway 5."

"How long will that take us?" Karen asked.

"Four or five hours, unless we run into more road blocks."

Five and a half hours later, they reached the Boender farm. Joe stood to one side as hugs and laughter mingled with tears were passed around.

"I'm guessing you are Karen's father," George said, as he held out his hand to Joe. "Welcome."

Joe shook his hand and looked at Grandma Rose. "You look the same as ever." He said.

Grandma smiled and said, "Well, I'm not as spry as I used to be, but I'm doing fine." Grandma turned to the young blonde girl, who was standing by her. "This is your daughter, Grace."

Grace was shy, but she went to Joe and hugged him. He accepted her hug with tears in his eyes.

"I was so afraid that you would run out of fuel." George said.

Jack answered, "We bought diesel fuel, just before we crossed the Mississippi River. It was a few miles later that cars and trucks and debris were flying everywhere. People were screaming and crying. It was awful! We were toward the end of the multi - vehicle accident. To avoid crashing, I drove into the ditch for a bit, then returned to the exit. My GPS didn't work, so we just rode west and a little south."

Joe face looked troubled. He said, "I don't know where to go."

George spoke to Joe, "All of our beds are being used, but you can sleep in the barn, if you want. We will need a lot of help with milking, since we don't have electricity. I would like you to stay and be our hired man."

Joe took his handkerchief from his pocket, wiped a tear from his face and blew his nose. Joe's voice was husky as he said, "Thank you very much."

Jack said, "I need to get home and see my folks. . . . I haven't talked to them for two days."

"Your dad was here this morning. He was checking to see if we heard from you." George said. "Take Ryan's bike and you will go faster."

Ryan nodded his head in approval.

Jack waved goodbye as he hurried home to his parent's house on Ryan's bike.

Grandma Rose said, "If anyone is hungry, I put another pot of soup to simmer on the stove. My stove works because it is propane."

Betty, George, Ryan, Sally, Grace, Ann, Karen, and Joe followed Grandma Rose into her little house. Since no one had eaten since breakfast and it was now after 4 p.m., the soup smelled especially good.

They all bowed their heads for grace as George thanked God for their safety. The soup was delicious.

Chapter 34

ONE YEAR LATER
It seemed ironic that Independence Day, July 4, was the birth of our nation and now the rebirth of it, since it was the same day that the electricity was eliminated and the same day it was restored. Did someone plan for this to happen on the same day of the next year?

The Boender family survived!

It was a year to remember and a year to forget, but it can never be forgotten. The people are different. People now have a deeper appreciation of themselves and the environment. They even feel differently about the machines that made their lives less labor intensive.

It was still difficult to learn about family and friends, since communications are in the infant stage. It was terrible to learn that more than 50% of people didn't survive.

Perhaps, someday, Sally and Grace will be able to travel to the Chicago area, when train tracks are operational. Coal is again taken from the open pit mine that was the Wilcox Coal company. Both coal and wood are burned to produce steam for the trains.

No one in Iowa knows who is running the new government, because of rumors and no way to hear the news.

In November, a young man, who was traveling west to his parents' home in Nebraska, stopped at the Boender farm to rest. Grandma gave him some soup that she always seemed to be cooking. He told her of a rumor that New York City and Washington D.C were bombed with nuclear weapons. Then, the electrical system failed as one by one the grids fell like dominoes.

Good things also happened during the last year. Karen and Jack got married in September in the little Methodist church in Forest Grove. In the attic, of the main Boender home, they found Karen's mother's blue Amish wedding dress. Karen was grateful to wear this dress, when she married Jack. Joe, her father, stood beside her to give her his blessing. Betty was happy to decorate her house with the perennial flowers and even used her best dishes for the reception.

Betty even made the cake, which was baked in Grandma Rose's oven. Jack's parents furnished eggs for the cake. All the chickens, that were not laying eggs, were slaughtered for meat for the reception. They canned the excess chickens. Now, the corn that was fed to the chickens could be used for corn meal instead of chicken feed. Canned and fresh vegetables were added to the menu. Esther, Grandma's friend from church, gave Grandma some sour dough starter to make bread, since the yeast was gone.

Just before the wedding, since the Boenders were almost out of coffee grounds, Grandma gathered chicory flowers from the ditch in front of the property. She dried these and added them to the remaining grounds. It still didn't taste right, so Jack's mother contributed coffee grounds and two new pots of real coffee were made for the wedding reception. When the coffee was gone, Betty still had her instant coffee to use. Grandma said that she was just going to drink tea from now on for her morning beverage.

Karen and Jack moved into Jack's house with his parents, but they were frequent visitors to the Boender farm. They usually used the bicycles to get around, but Karen isn't doing that any-more. She is afraid of falling, since she is seven months pregnant.

The only person to gain weight, besides Karen, is Betty. She wasn't afraid to eat, even though the others were cautious with the food supply. Now, there is plenty to eat because the new garden is growing from the seeds that were carefully saved from last year's produce. Soon, they will be able to buy groceries from the HyVee grocery store in Albia.

Last year more labor was needed for everyday life. Since the electricity is working again, Betty appreciates her microwave and automatic washer and dryer that George got to work for her.

The well is still working, but water is still boiled for half an hour before it is used for food or drinks. Three drops of bleach per quart of water are also used to destroy any pathogens that may have gotten into the water supply. Rain water was caught in the large tubs that the Boender's owned, but that water was also boiled before use.

The septic tank is still functioning. In the winter, they gath-ered water from the pond. A bowl was placed in the sink, to catch hand – washing water. This was used to flush the toi-lets. They limited their showers, unless they had rain. Baby wipes were used for cleaning themselves when it was too cold to bathe in the creek. Karen asked Grandma Rose to save some baby wipes for her baby.

They ran out of tooth paste, so they used baking soda to brush their teeth, but it tasted awful. Hopefully, they will soon be able to buy real tooth paste.

Clothes were washed by hand until George traded some milk and cream for an old wringer type washing machine with a crank handle. The Amish owner had died, so her son traded it to the Boender family. George put a rope between two trees as a place to dry their clothes. Jack also tied a rope between two poles at his family home. He teased Karen that now they had a solar dryer.

Jack's mother did the washing and drying of clothes, now that Karen is expecting a baby. They had always wanted more children, but only had Jack. They are exuberant because of their expected grandchild.

Everyone was careful with the laundry soap and washed white clothes first, then light colored clothes and then the dark work clothes in the same tub of water with the same detergent. Then they used another tub, with clean rinse water, to rinse. They were afraid that they may have to learn to make soap from ashes and animal grease.

No one knew what happened to Ellen and her husband in California or Sally and Grace's families from Illinois. Karen knew that Ellen, the woman who raised her, would have been excited about her wedding and expected child.

Ann and Sally live in a house not far away with an elderly woman. They do her housework and make her meals, but also go together to work as a nurse and nurse aid. They have even made house calls, when their patients' family supply gas for the Volkswagen. Gas has been syphoned from abandoned vehicles, but the women ask no questions about where the patient's family get their gas.

Ann and Sally both wear the masks, that they had from the Covid 19 epidemic a few years earlier, when they see patients. Not only does it help with sanitation, but the stench from the countryside has been very bad from the unburied people and animals. A little Vicks in the masks helps to hide the unpleasant odors.

Fortunately, a local pharmacy bartered medical items and medicine to the nurse and nurse aide before looters found the pharmacy. What supplies the women have available to them remains secret.

Grace lived with Ann and Sally, until she got married to Ryan at Christmas. It was a good time to celebrate the love of two young people and also the love shown by God sending his son as a babe in Bethlehem.

It was a small wedding because Grace had not heard from her family. Sally was her maid of honor; both Karen and Ann were her bridesmaids. Jack was the best man and two neighbor men were groomsmen.

Ryan cut down a pine tree, which was decorated with ornaments his family owned. There were no lights on the tree. People used to put candles on the trees, but George was afraid of fire. Grandma Rose found some white draperies in the attic and made Sally's dress.

Shortly after the wedding, they ran out of toilet paper. Kleenex, paper towels and napkins were used indoors but the women never flushed them down the toilet because they were afraid that the pipes would be clogged on their way to the septic tank. Instead, the used papers were put into a waste basket and later burned. Dishwater and handwashing water were saved in bowls and used to flush the indoor toilets.

George and Ryan built a small building for a privy, but the women can still use the indoor bathroom. Joe was especially glad to have an outdoor privy, because he hated to go into the house just to use the toilet.

A bedroom was made in the barn for Joe. He liked his privacy. Except on the coldest days, when he slept in George's house, he was comfortable in what he called his "log cabin". Ryan and Jack added logs to the inside walls to insulate them. The women had scrubbed the area and put small rugs down on the floor. It even had curtains on the room's one window. Joe helped milk the cows and was a handy man around the Boender farm.

A few cows were sold, or rather bartered, to the Amish for milk and beef. Milk was boiled in the tank that had been used for milk storage when large semi-trucks delivered milk to the dairy. This milk was taken to the Amish farmer's market, that was held in Moravia, every Tuesday and Friday via the old truck that Ryan owned. The old truck was so useful.

Money wasn't very useful last year. No one knew what inflated dollars were worth and you can't eat money. Most of the milk and cream were bartered, but dollars will soon be the best trading commodity.

Grandma Rose remains as busy as ever. She found a flannel blanket in the attic that she cut into squares and hemmed for diapers for Jack and Karen's baby.

Besides sewing by hand, Grandma sits in her recliner and reads. Last year, when the television wasn't running; the whole family did more reading. They played games, especially card games. The young people are looking forward to using a computer and cell phone again, but the systems to use them are not yet completed.

Last year, the garden yielded: carrots, beets, squash, turnips, and white and sweet potatoes. These hardy vegetables were stored in the two root cellars that Ryan and Jack each made on their respective farms. Tomatoes, peas, and green beans were canned.

The men butchered a bull calf last fall. Some of the meat was grilled over an open fire in the yard. The grilled meat tasted so good! Grandma, Karen, and Ryan and Jack's mother were happy to help can the meat and share it.

Since the bull calf didn't need the milk anymore; the cow was traded to an Amish family with ten children. The Amish father and his teenage sons brought their horse and plow, and not only prepared the soil for planting, but also planted the corn and soy bean field this spring.

Of course, everyone still has a lot of adjusting to do, since it has only been a few weeks since the electric power was restored. Now some machines need new parts, in order to function again.

Grandma Rose often says that the many coincidences that allowed Karen to find her sister, Grace, and their father, Joe, - was God's grace. It is also God's grace that they were led to prepare for the electrical failure.

Other Books by Darlene Miller

RV Chuckles and Chuckholes

The Confessions of Happy Campers

Darlene Millers' book, RV Chuckles and Chuckholes- The Confessions of Happy Campers, is full of amusing anecdotes, jokes, adventures, and pot-hole experiences while traveling in an RV (recreational vehicle) throughout the USA and Canada. It includes stories about sleeping in a real bed when visiting relatives, how to get rid of your husband (for a little while), and special RVers, such as the gentleman who had a complete heart transplant 19 years previously. She shares Rving tips and RVers secrets. She gives on-the-road advice and relates off-the-road experiences. Witty, poignant, and insightful, this book gives you a delightful view of life on the roam.

More RV Chuckles and Chuckholes

More Confessions of Happy Campers
Darlene Miller has a second book about the RV lifestyle, which
is full of amusing anecdotes, jokes, adventures, and chuckhole
experiences while traveling throughout the USA and Canada.
It includes stories about the search for the white Kermodei bear
in British Columbia; how to stay in touch with your grandchil-
dren while traveling and bond with other RVers while parked
in the desert around Quartzsite, Arizona. Guest contributors
write about the quest for New Mexican chilies; what happens
when the windshield breaks in the middle of traffic on the San
Francisco Bay Bridge; or how to RV when you are born with
no mechanical genes.

The Search for Grandma Sparkle

A novel About the Mysterious Disappearance of a Rural Senior Citizen

When granddaughter Sarah learns that her grandmother Opal and niece Jessica are missing, she decides to search for her. When the car is found with two flat tires, Sarah and her boyfriend from college travel up and down the rural roads and creeks of southern Iowa to look for her missing relatives. Because of the storm that Saturday night, would they seek shelter in an abandoned barn, house, or maybe even a coal mine whose opening has been uncovered? Were they abducted? Who would have a grudge against the gentle woman who only tried to help people through her church's SPARKLE Club?

Elijah and Emma Meet Friends and Visit History

A Story Book to Color

Instead of sitting in a classroom, Elijah likes to "do stuff." His grandmother helps the family to participate in reenactments and living history events where he and his sister Emily can experience the lifestyles of early America and the Civil War era. "To read about the reenactment of history is fascinating, to color the pages is to bring the story to life. Elijah and Emma Meet Friends and Visit History is truly one of a kind, encouraging people of all ages to seek out reenactments and places of historical value. Elijah and Emma Meet Friends and Visit History could only become priceless as the years pass."
Joan Pomeroy Author

Callie and Natalie's Dutch Family History

Callie and Natalie wear period dresses as they accompany Grandma Darlene Miller to learn about their fourth, fifth, and sixth great-grandparents who arrived in Pella in 1847. Other true Dutch stories are about great-grandparents who immigrated in the early 1900s. They see, hear, and taste "all things Dutch" as they travel through Pella.

www.ingramcontent.com/pod-product-compliance
Lightning Source LLC
Chambersburg PA
CBHW072125090426
42739CB00012B/3063